Ruth Livingston Hill

The *Jeweled* Sword

HARVEST HOUSE PUBLISHERS
Eugene, Oregon 97402

JEWELED SWORD

Copyright © 1955 by Ruth H. Munce
Published by Harvest House Publishers
Eugene, Oregon 97402

ISBN 0-89081-565-8

Printed in the United States of America.

~~~~~~~~~~~~~~~~~~~~~~~~~~~~~~

Other Books By
Ruth Livingston Hill

~~~~~~~~~~~~~~~~~~~~~~~~~~~~~~

Bright Conquest
The Homecoming
Morning Is For Joy

The Jeweled Sword

CHAPTER I

A split second before the crash Dave Truscott caught a glimpse of the girl who was driving the convertible.

Automatically he jammed on his brakes to avoid piling up on the two cars already tangled, for it was the hour of the home-going traffic rush. A crowd gathered instantly. Most people made for the wrecked car, a shabby jalopy. Its only occupant, a girl, lay twisted grotesquely along the front seat.

The accident was all the fault of the convertible. Its pretty driver still sat at the wheel, as if stunned by what had occurred. Her beautiful dark blue eyes, wide with horror, cast appealingly about among the crowd as if searching for a sympathetic face. She was a dainty, delicate little thing and Dave found himself resenting for her the curses of the bystanders. She was dressed exquisitely and she looked as if she had lived a sheltered life. She certainly hadn't planned to hit the other car. Why make it any harder than it was?

Dave opened his door. A glance toward the other car showed that kind hands were caring for the victim there, wrapping her in a warm robe, twisting a tourniquet about her bleeding arm. A black suit-jacket and a thin black purse had slid out. Somebody picked them up and brushed them off. A teacher's record book and a sheaf of papers with painstaking scrawls on them were being trampled in the mud. A dog-eared arithmetic was standing on end, its fractions exposed.

7

How suddenly the details of a private life had been brought into the notice of the general public!

The injured girl looked young, and very thin. Her face was ghastly white, except for an ugly red streak making its way across her cheek. Was she dead?

Throngs of gapers, greedy for horror, craned their necks to get a better view, so as to be first to tell their neighbors that night how badly mangled the victim was. They flung darts of denunciation at the lovely girl sitting safely in her handsome shiny car.

Dave wished the ambulance would arrive. When the injured girl was gone, most of the crowd would lose their interest.

The girl in the convertible had covered her eyes now from the sight of blood, and she was shaking nervously from head to foot. Poor kid! She didn't know what to do. Impulsively Dave took a step toward her. Nobody was doing anything for her and she needed help as much as the other one, only in a different way. Dave straightened his shoulders. As he drew near all he could see of her was a pert skullcap of purple velvet, a blond curl or two, and a soft little ear to which clung a tiny, sparkling, jeweled sword.

Suddenly, as if she had been watching for him, the girl raised her head, and her eyes met his. There was something compelling in their mysterious depths which drew Dave on. He had the strange sensation that he ought to drop on one knee to offer his aid, as if here was a girl the like of which he would never meet again.

As he gazed at her sympathetically, two big tears filled her eyes. She shuddered again and put out her hands as if to push from her the sight of the bloody heap in the jalopy.

Dave took a step nearer.

"It's tough," he said gruffly. "But don't take it too hard. She may have just surface cuts. Sometimes they look worse than a serious wound. Got your license?" He asked her more to distract her thoughts than because he wanted to see the license.

"I—I hope so," murmured the girl shakily. With a helpless gesture she held out her purse to him. It was a smart-looking kid affair with the initials D R D on it, done in gold. The bag and the silk suit she wore were the color of purple grapes, and set off gorgeously the bright gold of her hair.

Hesitatingly Dave took the handbag, aware of the girl's mute trust in him. All at once his hands seemed large and clumsy and he wished he had spent more time scrubbing up before he left the office. The boss had given him a lot of dusty old papers to sort and his nails felt gritty from them.

Awkwardly he unfastened the clasp and held the bag open toward its owner, but she made no move to take it.

"Oh, won't you see if it's there?" she pleaded like a child. "I'm shaking so I can't hold anything."

Reverently, Dave put his hand into the soft fragrant recesses of the bag and drew out a fat leather wallet.

"Would it be in this?" he asked. His voice was gentle.

"I guess so," she responded tearfully. "I can't seem to think. I'm so upset. Oh, will they put me in jail? Or—or—oh, what do they do? Suppose that girl *dies?*" She shuddered again and a deep sob shook her.

"Let's not worry about that yet," said Dave reassuringly. "What happened, anyway? Did the sun blind you?"

"I—I guess that must have been it. I swear I didn't see a car coming. I looked both ways. I—I'm *sure* I did, just before I reached over to light my cigarette."

"Didn't you see that the light was against you?" he probed.

If he was to be any help to her he might as well get things straight right at the start.

"Light? Oh, no, I didn't. That is, I don't know as I even saw there was a light. Oh-h, what will they do to me?"

Dave ignored a prick of irritation. The girl didn't seem to give a thought to the fact that it was the other one, not she, who was hurt. That would come to her later, and surely it would shock her.

Soon the police arrived to take over and then an ambulance screamed its approach. Dave scribbled down the girl's address from her license. Her name was Darla Ray Dartman and he noted that she lived in a better than average apartment house fronting a large city park. He returned the card to her and stood by to help in case he was needed.

It seemed that he was, for in response to every question the officer asked, she turned to Dave childishly, expecting him to answer for her. It was difficult to reply honestly without involving her inextricably.

"You'll have to come down to headquarters," the police ordered sternly.

The girl wilted and turned once more to Dave.

"Oh!" she wailed. "I won't know what to do. You'll come with me, won't you?"

An appeal in her tone that brought him strange bewildering pleasure made Dave respond.

"Of course. Be glad to!" and then he wondered why he had let himself in for such a lot of bother. There might be need to appear in court. His boss wouldn't like that; he would tell Dave that he should have had sense enough to keep clear of an accident in which he was not directly involved. Still, he found himself reluctant to leave a girl who seemed to depend so much on him.

The convertible was damaged too badly to run. Both cars

would have to be towed in. Dave helped the girl into his own third-hand jalopy, taking satisfaction in the fact that, in spite of its age, it was immaculate, inside and out. It was the first piece of property that Dave had ever owned and he took the greatest care of it. Years of watching his family neglect what they owned had made him determine to do the opposite.

The police gave a nod to Dave and they set out. Qualms arose in Dave's mind again as they proceeded. Why had he done such a crazy thing as to befriend a perfect stranger? Why hadn't he let the girl look after herself? If she was old enough to drive a car, she was old enough to manage her own difficulties. Then he glanced down at her and found her big eyes upon him gratefully. Something warm surged in his heart and he smiled. She returned his smile with a little wistful drooping one that seemed to claim his sympathy.

Her soft silk gown, her slender, graceful ankles, her little kid-shod feet, the very tilt of her patrician head all spoke of the things that Dave had always longed for, the gracious cultured life that he had read about and never experienced, a life in which there was order and plenty, and peace, and someone to care. His heart sank. If she knew what his life was like, would she want to be friends with him?

He looked down at her again and found that she had buried her face in her hands and was shaking with sobs once more. He wanted to put his arm around her, and comfort her.

"Oh, I say!" he spoke in a voice husky with sympathy. "Don't let it get you down. Things may not be so bad. By the way, will your folks worry?"

She shook her head.

"Nobody cares what I do or knows when I come in," she said. Her tone was sad and bitter.

"I see." Dave's heart went out to her all the more. "That's

tough." He paused and added, "I know!"

She looked up with a quick, keen glance and seemed to move a little closer to him. Dave took a tighter grip on the wheel. That little wistful leaning motion toward him stirred him as nothing had ever stirred him before. He found himself almost glad that she was in trouble so that he could help her. It didn't make sense.

Her eyes met his again and then drooped shyly.

"Don't be frightened," he reassured her comfortingly.

"What do I do when we get to the police station?" she asked tremblingly.

"Just answer the questions they ask. Tell the truth. That will never hurt you. Do you have liability insurance?"

"I think so."

"With what company, do you know?" He knew the question was useless as soon as he asked it. She was too much of a child to have paid any attention to business matters. She needed someone to look after her.

A sudden thought pierced him: perhaps she was married. He glanced down at her left hand. No ring there. Good! That gave him more right to look after her himself. It was a wonder, though, that somebody hadn't snatched her up before this.

Dave felt quite mature in comparison with her apparent immaturity, although at first impression he had taken the girl to be older than himself. Perhaps she had had a lot of trouble. That always aged a person. She looked very young and unprotected now, sitting there beside him so forlornly.

"Look in your wallet and see if you don't have an insurance identification card," he commanded. "The accident should be reported immediately."

It took her only a second to riffle through the cards in her fat wallet and produce the right one. She wasn't so helpless, after all! She had just been upset before, too shaken to think clearly.

But at the police station she seemed quite frightened again and leaned on Dave to answer for her. It was pleasant to feel that he was important to her. He had felt unnecessary most of his life.

He looked proudly down at her. She wasn't crying now. She was actually smiling pitifully at one of the officers. A dimple stole timidly into the smile and then vanished. She was marvelous! Her name suited her, too. Darla! She was a little darling. And the rest of her name reminded him of the bright sparkle of the scintillating jeweled swords in her ears. He studied her a moment, delighting in her loveliness. He saw that other men in the room were noticing her, too. But she was his to protect and care for, at least for the time being. Just then she glanced up and saw that there were eyes upon her. Her own dropped and she blushed modestly. Brother, what a girl!

The session at the police headquarters was gruelling. After it was over, Dave led Darla back to his car, marveling that she had stood it all so well. They started for her home address.

"I'm so ashamed to have taken your time like this," murmured Darla as they wound their way through twilight traffic that was beginning to head for evening entertainment.

It was May and darkness approached slowly as if to give the lazy spring days as much time as possible.

"Don't give it a thought," Dave assured her. "It was a pleasure, really." He was trying to think of some way in which to prolong the time with her. Suddenly he was aware that he was hungry, and she must be, too. It was long past dinnertime. But he had only a dollar and a half in his pocket. What should he do? He would have given anything to be able to take her out, but he couldn't ask a girl like Darla to a third-rate sandwich joint such as he generally patronized. Even at such a place it was scarcely possible to feed two adequately on a dollar and a half. He began to grow hot all over. He had a feeling that Darla was waiting for him to ask her to stop somewhere for something to eat. No doubt she would refuse even if he did ask her. She was too nice a girl to consider going out to dinner with a young man she did not know. Yet what if she were counting on his kindness as a sort of introduction and she accepted? His hands on the wheel perspired. He drove slower.

The silence grew embarrassing. He imagined that Darla was laughing at his dilemma though she couldn't possibly know what he was thinking! Well, some day maybe they would laugh together over this.

He finally decided that it was out of the question for him to try to buy a dinner, so it would be best to say nothing about it.

He soon drew up at the handsome stone apartment house. "I'll stop at Municipal Hospital tonight and see how that girl is getting on," he promised. But at mention of the other girl Darla only put up her hands to her face and shuddered. Dave felt guilty that he had brought up the subject again. Darla was still too upset to talk about it. He hastened on. "And I'll check on your car the first thing in the morning and let you know what has to be done to it. You had better call your insurance company too."

Darla raised her head again, pitifully.

"Oh, I'm so grateful to you!" She broke into a smile then.

Her dimple danced and it made Dave's heart dance as he helped her out of the car.

She paused just an instant and put out her hand. It felt like fresh rosebuds in his. She leaned toward him the least bit and spoke in a low voice. "You're *terrific!*" she said, and smiled again. "Thank you *so* much!" Then she left him.

Dave stood looking after her, trying to get his breath. She liked him! He straightened his tie and stood a little straighter. For the first time in his twenty-two years he decided that life was worth living.

With quickened step, he strode round his car and got in, starting off on the road toward home with his heart still pounding. He had forgotten all about the girl who lay unconscious in Municipal Hospital.

CHAPTER II

DAVE DROVE home excitedly. When he reached the top of the steep hill on which the house stood, and maneuvered the difficult turn between the big stone gateposts, relics of the horse and carriage days of the old mansion, he remembered the girl in the hospital.

With an exclamation of impatience at his own stupidity, he inhibited the impulse to put his foot on the brake. Instead he kept on up the drive and parked under the dilapidated porte-cochere. No use to go back now before he had fixed dinner. He could go back later. The ten miles extra wouldn't be any shorter if he took them now, and anyway he had nothing else to do tonight. Dad would fuss at his going out again but he was used to that.

As he opened the car door, with care lest he bump the stone wall and spoil his good repaint job, he gazed from force of habit at the dark plumy pines beyond the slope of the hill. He had always loved those pines in the distance, much as he despised the rest of the place in which he lived.

In the ten years before his mother gave up trying to make her marriage a success, and went away to die alone, she had made a deep impression on her son. Whenever Dave saw anything beautiful, especially in nature, it always stirred in him a longing for his mother. He never heard any good of her, only bitter recriminations, but he had always secretly felt that there must have been lovely things about her, in spite of what his father said.

The sun was setting behind the pines now, flinging its streamers this way and that in lavish abandon. One was curved, like the rubied sword in Darla's ear. Darla was like the sunset, gorgeous, and set apart beyond one's possessing, perhaps, but still greatly to be admired in one's secret heart. Dave always felt rested after a gaze at the pines and the sweep of orange and gold that wove itself between them. The bright rays seemed like kindness gently stealing through the unloveliness of life.

But after a moment he turned resolutely back to the house. He dreaded to look at the house and the unkempt grounds around it. It epitomized all that he hated. It sat in isolation on the summit of a hill like a fat old faded beauty in a rickety rocker, deluding no one but herself about her age. The house was built of dark granite, solid and dull. Every vestige of paint had long ago worn off the trim. A section of porch railing had fallen back upon itself and it hung toward the ground like a torn cuff. The blinds were splintered and sagging. One had flopped shut over an unused upper window. It always reminded Dave of Aunt Amelia's left eyelid that drooped at unexpected moments. More than one window was broken; old newspapers, yellowed now, were still filling the holes where someone had stuffed them one cold winter day. Weeds ranged forlornly everywhere. A gaunt dirty hen took her way painstakingly down the shaky back steps to make one last try at scratching for something worthwhile among the sparse gravel left in the walk. A deathly stillness held the place in thrall, though Dave was quite sure his father must be around somewhere, and probably Aunt Amelia too, poking about in the oversized kitchen getting together a meal for herself and her grumpy husband when he should return from gathering the eggs.

Dave hated the whole menage. Once more he gave a wistful glance at the glory, beyond and above the ruin of earth, and sighed. He didn't give much thought to a God. He supposed there must be one up there somewhere, a God who had given a flip to start things going and then had gone off to some other concern and left earth to run itself, into destruction if it chose to! That was the sum of what Dave's father believed and the son had never had cause to question it. He knew his mother had believed in a God who cared. But of course that was plain silly. Look at life; there was proof enough. As for his aunt's type of religion, he despised it. She always went to church, sick or well, and tried to drag her husband with her. She would miss her meals before she would miss a church meeting. But when she came home it seemed to him that she practiced all the things the minister must have said not to do. There wasn't a sharper tongue in the countryside, nor a person who could hold a more bitter grudge.

Dave's face grew hard again at thought of her and his lip curled in scorn. He gave a slam to the car door and the old car seemed to shudder like a patient horse that had to endure the lash.

A shuffling step sounded around the corner of the wide porch and a stooped white-haired figure edged slowly into view.

He looked like a man of eighty, so bent and trembling he was, so uncertain on his feet, so dependent on his gnarled cane. Only his eyes still blazed with energy, beautiful, shiny, dark eyes like Dave's, under brows still youthfully black.

"Hunh, Dad," mumbled Dave in dismal greeting as he strode past his father and stamped up the stairs.

The decrepit man looked as if he had been struck, and not

unexpectedly. The bitter expression deepened on his lined face. But instead of staring angrily after Dave, he lifted his trembling fist and shook it viciously toward the kitchen window. His weak muttering lips bared in a snarl of hate and something like a growl sounded between his teeth. He held the look as if to let it reach its victim and do its work. Then his arm dropped impotently and he started the long slow trek to the third floor.

He could hear Dave slamming saucepans and opening cans in the dreary third-floor back room they had made into a sort of kitchen. By the time his father reached there, Dave was already putting some food on the table.

"Humph!" grunted his father lowering himself painfully into his chair. "Canned stew again! How delightful!" He said it sourly, with a sarcastic edge to his voice. "Let us be grateful for canned stew every night, I suppose. Don't they sell anything else at the stores any more?" His tone of voice was deadly. "This bread is five days old, too. I suppose you prefer it that way? You couldn't take time to stop and get some?"

Dave checked an angry retort. "There was an accident," he tersely explained.

His father waited, eager to hear more. When no more was forthcoming, he finally growled, "Were you mixed up in it?"

"No."

The old man cast a hard look toward his son. It was bad enough to put through the interminable hours alone every day without a human soul to speak to, but it was inexcusable that his own son would not vouchsafe him the pleasure of hearing a bit of news of the outside world.

The pigheaded, selfish pair who lived in the main part of the house, would never bother to speak or make life pleasant for him in any way. If that husband his sister had married in desperation had only half the sense of an ape, life would be more bearable. Things were even worse since the radio was out of order. Nothing to hear, no one to talk to, eons of emptiness! But he kept his lips closed. Others might complain of their lot, not he. It was part of his code to take what came and say nothing. The world was unjust to him, but the thing was to take it, and show himself more heroic than the next one who might murmur. He chewed hard on a piece of tough meat. That was unfair, too, that at his age, when he should be having nourishing food to try to recover from the three strokes he had had, that he must subsist on what a stripling could provide him. At fifty he should now be in his prime, still earning a good living and taking care of himself and a family. Instead, he was a pauper! Finished! A ruin! It was certainly through no fault of his own. If his sister hadn't acted like a fool, he would have had plenty. Everything was unfair, and he had happened to get the worst deal of all. If they didn't let such pigheaded idiots run the government, things might have straightened out long ago. But there was so much bribery, corruption, injustice. What a mess the world was in! Still he said nothing. He chose to keep the bitter fires inside his heart, bottled up. They could burn hotter that way.

Dave got up to get more stew. He, too, sighed in silence. He had thought of trying various lines of conversation but had discarded each one as a subject likely to stir up argument or draw on himself a long harangue. Silence was not exactly pleasant, but it was the lesser of two evils.

He glanced at his father's plate.

"More, Dad?" He tried to say it kindly. He dreaded to open the way even so slightly, for the rebuke that was sure to come.

"Not of this stuff!" grumped the man, wiping his mouth. That was one good thing, at least, thought Dave. His father didn't slobber like some old men, nor drop things on his clothes like Uncle Harry. *He* was positively loathsome. Uncle Harry always had spots on his vest. Sometimes they looked actually moldy, they had been there so long. Dave's father used to be immaculately groomed. It was difficult for him even to shave now, his hands trembled so badly. But Dave felt there was no use offering to help, for he would only let himself in for endless tasks and tongue-lashings if he did. He had found out long ago that his father was all too ready to take advantage of him.

Dave gulped down his third helping and shoved back his chair. He had to get back to town and see how that girl in the hospital was doing. Not that he cared anything about the girl, but the thought of seeing Darla again was pleasurable. News of the girl would provide an excuse to talk to Darla.

He took his plate to the sink and rinsed it, drying it carefully. He emptied the rest of the stew into a smaller dish and set it in the noisy old refrigerator, then set to work scouring the pan in which he had heated it. Everything Dave did which had to do with his own things or his own work, he did with care. His shirts were always clean, although he had had to learn to launder them himself. He shaved at least once a day, sometimes twice, for his hair was dark. He always presented a well-groomed effect. On his dresser he had a photograph of his father at twenty. He had been a handsome lad, well-dressed almost to the point of being dapper. There was a lovely wave in his black hair and even in the picture his eyes seemed alight.

Dave knew that he resembled what his father had been. Perhaps he was not so handsome, but he was taller, his shoulders were broader and he had a more powerful build. Dave secretly worshipped that young man in the picture. It was the one thing about his family that he felt he could be proud of. His ambition was to be the man that the lad in the picture might have become. Dave was resolved never to get into such a situation as his father had. He would walk more circumspectly. He had a good job, he was bright, he worked hard, he would save his money, not vainly splurge, as he suspected his father of having done. Dave rarely dated. Girls cost too much, and you couldn't trust them. The girl he had met this afternoon, well, she was different. She was to be admired from afar. Very likely she would never look at him again. It would do no harm to worship at her shrine for a day or so.

He glanced in the mirror as he gave a last lick to the wave in his hair and straightened his tie to cover the worn place.

His father watched him with immobile countenance. The old man's heart sank. Another lonely evening! He knew the signs. Dave was going out. Well, of course he must. He was young. His father hadn't an idea whether he was spending his time with girls, or men, or what he was doing. Dave never offered to explain. But Dave needed fun. There wasn't much around this old place.

"Brought y' a paper," said Dave as he started out. "Guess I left it in the car. I'll throw it up to the landing."

He was gone. A swishy thud on the stairs told his father that the paper had reached its goal. That was some comfort. He had read all the literature the house afforded over and over. A man of his intellect had to have something to read or he'd lose his reason!

But why couldn't Dave have brought the paper all the way up? The boy didn't know what tremendous will power it took to manage even the five steps down to the landing and back. He had no inkling of the smothered terror that the very thought of that landing always brought to his father's mind ever since the time he had reeled and fallen there when that last stroke took him. He had lain there all day, unable to move or call. No one would have come had he called, for his sister and her husband never came near him, hadn't spoken to him for years. Since that awful day he had never gone up or down those stairs that he wasn't afraid, but he wouldn't tell Dave that. Let every man bear his own burden. Some day things might be made right and the world would know that he had suffered in silence. That was his philosophy, and he was proud of it.

He pulled himself to his feet, painstakingly reached for his cane, and made his slow, shuffling way to where the newspaper lay, with almost the same fierce desire that some men go for liquor. The newspaper would serve to turn his thoughts away from the old, worn, painful groove at least for a time.

While he was gone, a tawny gaunt insect stole out, its feelers waving, and made for the crumbs beneath the old man's chair. It ate in a leisurely manner. Jason Truscott would be too glad to sit down again, and too eager for the paper when he returned, to be concerned with insects and their meals.

Dave drove back to the city, his mind on the girl he had met that afternoon. It was hopeless, of course, for him to dream. A girl like that would be used to having a great deal of money spent on her, and he had none. But just to think of her made him feel glad all over. His present errand was for her. Plenty of people were hurt in accidents every day and he didn't go to see them. He knew it was extravagant for him to be using the gas to go back to the city that night, but if that other girl should die, Darla would be in a bad spot. He stepped harder on the gas, as if by reaching the hospital sooner he could keep the injured girl alive.

It was an enormous hospital and there was much red tape. After a long time a nurse came toward him.

"Is your name David?" she asked with a smile.

Puzzled, Dave assented.

"You may come with me. She is calling for you. She has been unconscious until now, but your coming may do her good."

"Calling for me!" exclaimed Dave. But the nurse was already on the way to the elevator and didn't hear him. Several other people were in there and he didn't like to discuss the matter. It would straighten out. Anyway, he was going to get to see her. That was more than he had hoped for. He would have something definite to tell Darla. And at least she wasn't dead.

He heard her moaning before he entered the room.

"Davey! Davey!" she cried weakly.

"Here's Davey," the nurse told her comfortingly, leading Dave up to the bed.

Chapter III

PEARL STREET was dark and narrow. It seemed lonely in spite of its thickly huddled houses. In the second floor corridor of number 202, the smallest, most tumbledown house of all, it was very dark. From the room at the far end of the hall came the sound of patient sobbing.

The man who lived in the front room on that floor heard it as he reached the top of the stairs and made the turn around the stair rail. He paused a moment. There was no light coming from under the crack of the door, but he was sure he heard someone speaking, so he went on. That lame boy was likely in pain again and his sister was trying to soothe him. She'd do better to put him in a crippled children's hospital for good. Then she'd be free to live her own life.

The sobbing sounded louder as he reached his door, and he went in hurriedly and slammed it to shut out the sound. There was no one in the corridor now to notice, but the sound of speaking in the back room continued:

"Please, God, take care of my sister. I think something's wrong. She never was late like this before. She knows I'm—h-hungry! An' she knows it's dark!" There was a long-drawn-out childish wail, softly muffled. Then the little voice continued.

"Oh, please, God, won't You send her back? Or send *some*body. I can't go to anybody but You to ask."

25

The crying went on, interspersed with desperate pleas, but the man in the front room had turned on his radio so that he wouldn't be bothered. The moonlight stole in and gently touched the boy's hair as if to let him know that he was not entirely alone any more, but his face was buried in his pillow and he was crying too hard to notice. It was a long time before the sobs grew less and sleep came and took the child and rocked him for an hour.

Then suddenly there came a knock at the door and the boy started up in fright.

Dave stared down in bewilderment at the features of the girl on the bed. Her head was bandaged and she was ghastly pale. She seemed scarcely to breathe, and her lips were white. He tried to imagine what she must look like when she was up and around. But he could find no faintest resemblance to anyone he knew.

"Here's Davey," the nurse repeated gently, her finger on the girl's wrist.

Weakly, the patient reached a groping hand and the nurse motioned to Dave to take it. With embarrassment he put his big hand about the girl's cold one and tried to give her a reassuring pressure. But she drew hers away.

"No!" she protested with an effort. "No! That's not Davey." Then she opened her eyes. "Oh, who are you?" she moaned.

Dave felt ashamed, as if he had unwittingly tried to trick the girl. The nurse was puzzled. Dave simply stammered, "Please don't be frightened. I'm just a—a friend—of the girl who—" he stopped for he wasn't sure that he should bring up the subject of the accident. He floundered and looked over to the nurse for help.

"Don't you know David?" she urged, still trying to fit him into the picture for her patient.

"No, that's not my Davey," said the girl. "Oh, I must go to him!" She tried to raise herself up.

The nurse held her down, soothing her.

"Not yet, Miss Wrenn. Just wait a little. Everything will be all right."

"No, it won't be all right. Not till I get home to Davey. He will be frightened." Her strength seemed to return in a measure as she forgot her own pain and weakness in concern for her Davey.

The nurse looked across at Dave now, as if he should be able to straighten out the tangle.

"Look here, Miss—Miss Wrenn, my name is David, but I guess I'm not the one you want. I came over to see what I could do for you. Who is Davey? Could I go and get him? Where is he?"

The girl looked steadily up at him, her vision clearing.

"He is my little brother. He is at home alone, and he's lame. He can't even get out of bed." Suddenly she looked wildly about her. "How long have I been here? It's dark, isn't it! Oh, my poor little boy! He can't even get up to turn on the light. And he must be starved! I *must* go. Oh-h-h!" She tried again to rise up but she gave a sharp cry of pain and sank back.

"Now listen, Miss Wrenn. You have a broken collarbone, and you must lie still, the doctor says. Why don't you let this young man see to your little brother?" The nurse flung a questioning look at Dave for confirmation. He nodded, at the same time wondering what he was in for now. But if a simple errand to comfort a little boy could settle the situation, he was glad to be able to be of help. It might serve also to bring about good feelings on the part of the girl so that she would not be so likely to bring a heavy suit for damages against Darla.

"Give me your address, Miss Wrenn. I will be glad to go and see your brother."

The girl looked at him uncertainly as if passing judgment on him, whether he was someone with whom she wanted to trust her brother or not.

"I don't like to bother you, a stranger," she said, politely. "Perhaps," she suggested, turning to the nurse, "someone from the Red Cross could go, or the welfare. But they would be strangers too, to Davey." The tears were very near to overflowing as she thought of her brother. "I'd call one of the other teachers but they all went on a picnic today and I know they wouldn't be home yet. There is no phone in the house where we live so I can't get the landlady. Oh, I should have planned for something like this!"

"Listen, Miss Wrenn," he said earnestly. "I wish you would feel you could trust me. I really would like to be the one to go and comfort him. I'll do for him just what you say. I've been lonely and in trouble myself more than once."

At that the girl on the bed measured him again with a long searching look. He held her gaze and looked steadily back at her. He had a feeling that she could see every thought he had. His eyes did not waver for he was sincere in his desire to help the poor little kid. There was only one thought he hoped she could not see and that was that he was here for the sake of another girl.

At last the patient smiled a little.

"I'll be very grateful, then, if you will take Davey something to eat and tell him I'll be home tomorrow. I guess he'll be all right alone tonight." Tears welled up again at the thought but she had made up her mind what was the right thing to do and she had herself under control now. She gave the address and a few instructions about what to do for the boy.

"There's some change to get milk. I think the drugstore on the corner will still be open. And would you mind calling me from there?"

She reached for her worn handbag, the one Dave had seen a woman pick up after the accident.

"No," he stopped her gently. "I have enough. Forget it. Let me help that much." How odd, he thought in passing, that he should be spending some of his scant funds on a strange little boy instead of on the girl in whom he was suddenly so interested. But as a matter of fact, he was actually spending it on Darla, for he had started out to do all this for her.

The patient thanked him.

"Tell Davey I'll be all right tomorrow!" was the girl's last admonition.

"You won't if you don't quiet down now," warned the nurse, waving Dave out.

"Oh, do you think I did the right thing?" The girl quavered nervously after Dave had gone.

"I think you did just the right thing," the nurse reassured her. "If he hadn't been an all-right young man he wouldn't have come here in the first place, let alone offer to go to your brother. I'm sure everything will be all right. Now you try to go to sleep."

Dave wound about through the city streets looking for the obscure address the girl had given him. He was torn between annoyance at himself for having walked into such a tangle, and a strange eagerness to get to the child. He found himself recalling lonely nights in his own boyhood, when his father and mother had quarreled and then both gone out and left him to cry himself to sleep. Why did parents bring children into the world if they weren't going to look after them? In this case it might not be the parents' fault. They might be dead. Then why did God, if there was a God, allow a little child to be left like this with nobody to look after him? What a muddle the world was!

He turned his headlights up to read a street sign. Pearl Street. At last. It looked like anything but a pearl. But maybe the street was like the oyster shell, ugly and dirty, and the pearl was hidden somewhere, brought into being by the very travail of the living beings in the street.

Well, he wasn't sorry he had got into this situation, not yet! Maybe he could do something to make life a little less impossible for other souls like Darla and the little boy and his struggling sister. He had a strange feeling, as he climbed the steep dark stairway, that he was at last on the threshold of real life, that something wonderful was about to happen, though how it could come out of a place like this was more than he could tell. It wouldn't of course. The wonderful thing might be the new friendship with Darla. Already he could see her beautiful eyes fill with grateful tears when he told her of this visit. Her heart would go out to the lonely, frightened little boy. She would be glad he had done this.

He climbed the creaking stairs and found the door at the back of the hall and knocked. It was then that Davey awoke with a start.

"Who's that?" he cried quaveringly.

"I'm a friend of Anne Wrenn's," answered Dave. He had

decided that it would be better to prepare the boy before
he went in. "Are you Davey?"

"Yes." The boy's voice sounded a little relieved.

"I have a message from your sister," went on Dave. "May
I come in?"

"Yes. Oh, sir," as Dave entered, "is my sister all right?"

Dave could not help noticing that the boy's first concern
was for his sister and not for himself. As he talked, telling
as little as he could of the details of the accident, he glanced
about.

The room itself was as barren and ugly as the ones in the
big old barnlike house in which he lived. But this one was
not even large. The walls were painted an ultra-bright blue
which made the cubicle look even smaller than it was.
There was scarcely room to walk between the pieces of
furniture that were fitted in like blocks in a child's puzzle.
But the furniture itself was handsome, most of it lovely an-
tiques. Twin walnut beds, beautifully carved, a crotch walnut dresser, as lovely as a painting, a drop-leaf table that
would have graced a mansion, and on the floor an exquisite, old, blue Chinese rug. Obviously the Wrenns must
have lived in better circumstances at one time. These things
suited the delicate features and sweet dignity of that girl in
the hospital. He found that he was not surprised at the fine-
ness of the furnishings, shabby as her outfit and the rest of
her surroundings were.

One wall was graced by a lovely painting, a calm lake
with a white sailboat moving peacefully across it. Near the
boy's bed was a good copy of Sallman's "Head of Christ."
Dave was not well trained in art but he recognized good
things. Some of the old furnishings that had been his grand-
father's were still in the big old house on the hill and even

in their state of deterioration they always inspired in Dave a certain respect.

Beside the boy was a table on which were ranged dozens of stiff blue cardboard airplanes of all sizes and kinds. They were neatly made. It must have taken hours of patient work to cut them out. Dave wondered whether they were done by the child himself or whether his sister had made them.

"Your sister had a little bump," he explained casually. "She said to tell you she would be all right tomorrow."

"Oh, you mean there was an accident?" cried the boy. "I want you to tell me," he said seriously, "just what happened, and how she is. I can take it. I was—well, I *was* crying a little, because I didn't know where she was. But if I *know* things, they aren't nearly so bad to stand. Then I can pray about them, you know."

"Oh?" Dave couldn't help smiling at the boy's ingenuousness. But he caught the little fellow looking at him keenly and he sobered.

"It's a big help to pray," went on the boy. "Then you don't have to worry over things."

"No? Well, maybe you have something there." Dave tried to pass off the remark and go on to other subjects but the boy was insistent.

"Do you pray about things?" he asked point blank.

"We-ell, no, I can't say I do," hedged Dave, "at least not what you would probably call prayer."

Davey looked troubled.

"Perhaps that's because you don't know yet who your Father is." The boy gave a flash of a smile, almost pityingly.

"Could be," responded Dave absently. He was busy fixing the milk and sandwiches that the sister had asked him to get, and he didn't want to be bothered with the child's philosophizing.

Davey waited a moment after Dave had put the food before him, then he said, "I want to thank you very much for doing this for me, and I want to thank my Father in Heaven, too, for sending you. Dear Father," he went on with closed eyes, "it was just like You to remember me and to answer my prayer when You knew I was frightened and hungry. I know You did it for Jesus' sake. Thank You. Bless this nice man, too, and please make Anne well. Amen.

"Now tell me about Anne and the accident, please."

Dave began in a pleasant conversational tone as if he were starting a story.

"Well, I was coming down Roosevelt Highway about five this afternoon when I saw that the convertible ahead of me was about to hit another car. I slammed on my brakes and got out. Your sister's car was battered a little and she was bruised. They took her to the hospital and I went over there this evening to see how she was. They made her stay in bed because it's not good for a person who has had a bad jarring to get up and go around right away." Dave had decided on the way over just about how much he would tell the little brother. "Your sister was awfully worried about you and I said I would come over and see to you."

The boy stopped chewing and looked squarely at Dave for several moments.

"You mean you did that, and you didn't ever know my sister before?"

"Why, yes," Dave shrugged smilingly. "I saw she was in a jam and there didn't seem to be anyone else to go. I wasn't busy tonight."

"I never knew anyone except my sister to be as kind as that." He shook his head slowly. "She is like that. But most people aren't." Then he looked Dave in the eyes again. "That's funny," he said, "that God would make you do that and yet you don't know Him." He took another bite of his sandwich but kept on shaking his head in wonder.

Dave shifted uneasily in his chair and grew red.

He started to say that nobody at all made him do it, but he didn't want to stir the child up to preaching again, so he got up and reached for the milk bottle.

"Have some more milk?" he suggested, although Davey hadn't yet finished what he had.

"Not yet, thank you," said the boy. "It all tastes very good." He smiled, another smile like a flash of light. "I was awful hungry."

"How old are you, Davey?" asked his visitor, trying to seem friendly.

"Almost nine. Anne was hoping I'd be well enough to take a ride out somewhere in the country on my birthday but I don't guess I will." He sighed.

"What has been your trouble?" asked Dave.

"Polio." He answered in a matter-of-fact tone, as if most boys had had something or other and it might as well be polio as anything. "My sister gives me treatment every morning and every night and I'm lots better, but I'm too big for her to carry and I can't walk down to the car yet. The doctor says if I keep on, though, that I might be able to get around by fall."

"That's tough!" said Dave. "I'll bet you used to like to play ball, too." Inwardly he felt the old familiar, sickening stab of frustration at the thought of another life ruined. Everything was unfair!

"Oh yes," shrugged the boy. "But it won't last forever. Of course God *could* heal me right now, but He hasn't. So Anne says I must have needed to learn a lot of patience. And she says, how would you learn patience if you didn't have something to practice being patient about?" He grinned sheepishly.

Dave listened to the boy's chatter absent-mindedly, wondering how to cheer him up. Wondering, too, how soon he could get away and call Darla. After all, she was the real reason he was here.

"Oh, you'll be around and playing ball yet," he said with more assurance than he felt, for it had been his experience that the worst, not the best, generally happened. He wouldn't say that to a little fellow, though. Time enough for him to find that out.

"Yes, I know," agreed the boy with unruffled calm. "I *hope* it will be down here, but of course I can play ball when I get to Heaven. No polio there!" he ended gleefully, then sighed a little wistful sigh.

"You're a brave kid," commented Dave. He had a defeated feeling as if he, at his age, ought to have more to give this child than the platitudes he was handing out to him. It was not exactly pleasant to find that the boy had more in the way of a philosophy to go on than he did. He studied Davey's earnest face and firm determined chin, his gray eyes so like his sister's, his straight neutral-colored crew cut. How wise of the sister to keep the boy looking boyish, even in bed. Dave had expected to find a frail looking, ill-groomed, pampered little fellow. He glanced at Davey's hands. They were sturdy and firm, as if they had often grasped a ball and bat. It was surprising to find him so tough and boyish, but his constant way of taking heavenly things into his calculations was contradictory. Dave couldn't make him out.

"No, I'm not really brave," acknowledged the child. "I was a chicken tonight when Anne didn't come home!" He swallowed the last bite of his sandwich and reached for the cookies Dave had brought him. "Say, have *you* had anything to eat?" he asked suddenly.

"Oh yes, I've had my dinner," Dave assured him, "before I left home."

"Where do you live?"

"Out in the country. Do you know where the Aeronautics Naval Research laboratory is?"

The boy brightened with interest. "I know where Bolling Field is."

"Well, the lab is just south of it and I live about two miles beyond there."

"That must be fun, to go by there every day and see the planes and things."

"I work there," said Dave.

"Ya do? Oh boy! What do you do?"

Dave smiled. "There is a small helicopter factory in connection with the research lab. I work there. I'm what they call a draftsman."

"What's that?"

"I draw designs and plans for parts. I am going to school one night a week, too, to learn more about aeronautics and other things."

"That would be hard work."

"Yes, it is. But everything is that's worth while."

"That's just what Anne says. I have to work hard at my spelling. I hate it. Anne says it's worth while but I don't see why."

Dave smiled understandingly. "I used to feel just the same way, kid. But I've found out it is worth it. I'm glad now I learned to spell. You know, it's a funny thing, but I happened to discover that that was the reason I got this job I have. Another fellow almost got it but he fell down on spelling."

"Good night! What does spelling have to do with helicopters?"

Dave laughed. "Doesn't seem as if it would, does it? But it's true." He gathered up the crumbs on Davey's table and stepped down the hall to the bathroom to wash the milk glass. It was a dreary place, this rooming house. Too bad the kid couldn't be outdoors a lot. Nobody could get well in a dark hole like this. The shadow that always lay over everything in Dave's world grew darker. Unfair! A nice kid like this one, still believing in a God, and yet what did God do for him? Nothing! It didn't make sense.

The shadow of that was on Dave's face when he came back into the room. But Davey's face was bright with welcome.

"I was just thinking how swell it was for you to come. It's been awful nice. I guess you—I suppose you—have a—a home, don't you? And a—family? They'll be expecting you?" Davey hesitated and stammered. His eyes fell shamefacedly. Then he looked up again, to see if Dave knew what he was trying to say.

"Oh, yes, they'll expect me some time or other," he answered carelessly. A bitter note was in his voice that Davey caught but didn't understand.

"Oh. I was afraid so." He sounded deflated, and his upper lip tried to settle down firmly on the lower, but it trembled and he didn't quite make it.

Dave looked up just in time to see it. "Why? What's the matter, young fella?"

Davey shook his head. "Nuthin'," he muttered discon-

solately, and gave a weak smile again. "I was just thinkin'
it would be nice if you could—I mean, will you—come back
sometime?" he added wistfully.

"Sure, I will," promised Dave without thinking. His main
aim was to keep the child satisfied and get away. It was already rather late to call Darla. "Sure, I'll be back and tell
you all about the new pocket helicopter."

Davey's eyes shone again for an instant. "Oh, boy!" Then
gloom settled once more and he said, reluctantly, "Well, I
guess you gotta go, dontcha? You better turn off the light.
The landlady fusses somethin' awful if we leave it on long,
evenings. She watches everything like that for fear it'll cost
her some money. I bet she wouldn't like to stay alone in
the dark, though." Davey's voice was thick with a smothered sob now and something made Dave withdraw his hand
from the light switch.

"Say, it *is* tough, isn't it! Would you—would she maybe
come up and stay with you? How about letting me call her
and ask."

"Who? Mrs. Pincheon? Not her, no sir! She doesn't like
it a bit that I'm here at all. It's only 'cause I'm lame and
can't get around to destroy things, she says, that she let
Anne and me come here at all. No, I'd rather be alone, even
without *God* than have *her* up here!" Davey groaned.

Dave hesitated. "I hate to go off and leave you, young
fella!" It didn't seem right to leave the boy without some
expression of commiseration.

"I'll—make out," responded Davey in a small shaky voice.

"Isn't there somebody else in the building who would
look in now and then? I saw a light under that front door
down the hall. Who lives there?"

"Just a man. He's been nice, sometimes. He brought Anne

candy twice and he wanted to take her to a show. But Anne doesn't trust him. That's why she always locks the door at night. Never mind, I'll be okay. Good night, and thank you again, Mister—what's your name?"

"Dave, just like yours." Dave smiled.

"Hunh! That's nice!" the invalid managed a little surprised grin and shut his lips tightly again as he waved Dave out.

Dave hurried down the creaky stairs and out to his car. He was only anxious to get to the nearest drugstore and call Darla before it was too late to call.

He drove two blocks and found a dirty little store with a telephone booth. He looked up the number with a thrill to think that in another moment he would be hearing Darla's voice again.

He dialed, and dialed, and dialed. But the Dartman phone did not answer.

CHAPTER IV

THE ELEVATOR at the Chez Villon never clanged. It never seemed to start or even to stop. It simply ceased to rise, then soundlessly disclosed an aperture from which its flawless passengers might emerge.

Darla Ray Dartman was one of those who emerged at the eleventh floor. She was humming a little tune, the very latest. She unlocked the door and gave a quick survey around her ultra-modern apartment. It was a habit she had acquired since she had lived in hotels and apartments. If anyone had been in the rooms she could sense it instantly. There was always some stray evidence, however minute. This time it was just as she had left it.

She yawned delicately and slid her little velvet cap from her sleek curls. She stepped out of her kid slippers, wiggling her toes in their sheer nylons, and strolled sinuously across the luxurious pile of the carpet, savoring each delicious step. She posed before the four walls of mirrors in her bedroom and stretched leisurely, watching with admiration the smart cut of her gown and the play of her own curves. Then she laughed, a long low laugh, musical but mirthless, turning her head to study her profile from each side as she did so. She laughed again, just to see her dimple appear. Then shrugging her pretty shoulders carelessly, she removed her dress. She wore no slip and she had to glance again at the dainty picture she made in her lacy black underwear. Her skin was exquisite. It was a great asset.

Complacently, she went to her kitchenette and began to

40

fix a fruit salad. She opened a baker's carton and got out two cinnamon buns, considered a third and replaced it in the carton reluctantly.

She set the food on a low table beside her black plush chaise longue, and switched on a TV program. As she ate, she watched with a critically expert eye the love-making of a blonde and an oil magnate. It was a clumsy performance in her estimation and she leaned over and changed to a newscast. She gave close attention to it, especially the foreign news.

The telephone rang as she finished her supper. She flitted with interest to answer it.

"Where on earth have you been, Darla Ray? I've been calling you ever since five-thirty."

Merta Pilchester had a high, hard voice, without overtones.

She wasn't pretty; her oval face was too stiff, and her teeth were too high, and discolored besides. But she was smart, in more ways than one. She wore clothes in a manner to make even Darla envious, and her mind was like a steel trap, said the men who took her out. None of them wanted her for a wife but she had money and position. She was stimulating for a few hours at a time, and *very* useful if there were axes to be ground.

Darla laughed. She often laughed. It was good practice.

"I found me a new cradle-baby," she gave a patronizing chuckle.

The girl at the other end of the wire made a sound of impatience.

"He's a lamb," went on Darla, ignoring her.

"Lambs don't produce," objected Merta. "What good is he?"

"You'd be surprised." Darla held her ground. "He will be useful. And is he ever good looking! A starry-eyed sucker! Black wavy hair and shiny eyes and the best pair of shoulders!"

"Lots of gold?" put in Merta.

"No," admitted Darla. "But that's his only fault. Could be remedied. Clothes would help."

"Where'd you get him?"

"At a bending party."

"Don't tell me you've joined the army of innocent by-standers."

"Far from it. This time I did the dirty deed myself. Limp body of girl. Blood stains. X marks the spot. Po-lice. All the gory details, plus new hound dog."

"Hound dog? I thought you called him a lamb."

"Not much difference, is there? Anyway, he's abject."

"Any likelihood of lawsuits?"

"Oh, could be. But I'm well covered. Up to $300,000. I should worry. What's on your mind, anyway?"

"Why, I called to let you know we have a date to-night. Yours is blind but he sounds good. Army Intelligence brass."

"Hunh! Where?"

"We'll make the rounds, probably. Pick you up at nine. Okay?"

"Fine. I'll see you."

An hour later, Darla set forth arrayed in sparkling blue, the color of her eyes. She made an exquisite picture and the army officer showed pleased surprise, as he smiled down into her innocent flowerlike face. She was a distinct contrast to the smart, homely Pilchester girl. She was like an exotic bloom beside a flowerless cactus. He had been informed of the financial and political power of the Pilchesters, and realized that for the sake of it his friend was willing to forgo looks and charm. After having met Merta Pilchester he had expected to find that his companion for the evening was cut off the same strip, not beautiful but not dumb. This girl, however, was a prize, very beautiful and certainly not dumb. She lifted her face to his with an eagerness that was both intriguing and flattering. The sparkle in her eyes was an intelligent sparkle which the rubied swords at her ears intensified. The evening promised pleasure.

"Oh, Colonel!" exclaimed Darla as they sat cosily drinking in a secluded corner of one of the most exclusive night clubs, "do tell me what it's like in Russia? Is it as bad as they say?"

She listened with the impersonal interest that a manly man enjoys when he is talking about his work, and the colonel couldn't help thinking how stimulating it would be to have a companion like this to go home to, someone who would care to hear about his work and could discuss it intelligently. She seemed to have an unusual love for her country, too.

Darla drank very little, just enough to make her a good companion through the small hours as they talked and danced. But he wondered the next day whether he had been as wise himself. He found he had a rather worse headache than usual after a gay night. He sincerely hoped that he had not talked more than he should. It had been a temptation to do so, since the girl was so interested. Most girls who were as beautiful as she, and danced so well, were not politically minded.

They dropped Darla at her apartment around five in the morning and she went to bed and slept soundly, so soundly that even the telephone did not penetrate her dreams. It was the sleep of one who had done a good day's work.

But the other girl involved in the accident slept fitfully. She woke every few minutes, in spite of the sedative they had given her. She dreamed that a strange man was entering Davey's room and that Davey was frightened.

Anne Wrenn was only twenty-one and the care of her little brother was a comparatively new responsibility that had been thrust upon her less than a year ago when her mother died. The brother and sister would have had enough to live on, with care and Anne's substitute-teaching job, if Davey had not contracted polio. That had taken all of the backlog of their mother's savings and now there was nothing but Anne's small salary to keep them. Davey still had to have massage treatments. Anne had learned to give them, and the doctor had hopes of his being able to walk again but he was forbidden to put his weight on his legs at all yet. Sometimes it seemed to Anne that the burden was more than she could carry. She came home so tired at night that, much as she loved her little brother, it took all of her will power to make herself go through the rubbing ritual and to talk gaily all the time for she had to make the evening a bright spot for the little boy who was alone all day. She would fall into bed afterwards, completely exhausted, wondering how on earth she could waken early enough to grade her papers and plan the work for the next day intelligently. She was thankful for the chance to substitute in a sixth-grade class. Besides providing for them now it might make an opening for her to get a regular job in the fall.

Anne had faced the problem of her own sorrow right at the start.

"I'm *not* going to feel sorry for myself," she determined. "God had some reason for this, that I'm too small and stupid to see, and He'll give me the courage it's going to take, and work that will make me think of somebody else's troubles instead of my own." Then along had come the illness to Davey! It nearly capsized her little vessel of life, but she rose bravely to meet the challenge, slowly realizing that it might be but the answer to her prayer.

But now this accident of hers. How could that possibly fit into the picture? Wasn't there some mistake somehow on God's part? This looked like the end of everything. She was restless, wanting to twist and toss. But every time she moved, the red-hot pain flared up again in her shoulder. She had asked the nurse what was wrong with her, for at first she had seemed to hurt all over. Unless a concussion showed up, she was told, the broken collarbone seemed to be the only injury besides various cuts and bruises. Still, even this would cut her out of several days' pay.

She had had hopes of finding some cheap room in the country, perhaps at a farm, where she could take Davey when school was over until the fall term started. He needed so very much to get out into the sunshine. He hadn't been outside the house for weeks. Some of her teacher friends at school would have been glad to take him riding, for a few of them owned cars, but he was too heavy for her to carry downstairs. The man in the front room at the rooming house had suggested taking them, and she had been greatly tempted to accept his offer, but she did not like the man's looks. He was not interested in her brother at all; that was obvious. He was only trying to make an impression on her and she did not care to be impressed. If she accepted favors from him she would be obligated to go out with him alone sometime and that she would not do. Still, Davey longed so to see the woods and grass.

Anne groaned. The woman in the next bed cursed. Anne was sorry she had disturbed her. She had forgotten that there were other patients in the ward.

What was she going to do for Davey if she couldn't go home tomorrow? She *must* go home. She tried tentatively to raise herself up in bed after the nurse went out again. The pain was frightful but she had to see whether she could possibly make it. She soon sank back, faint and dizzy. Well, perhaps if she got some sleep she would feel better tomorrow morning. Poor Davey. Did that young man go to him or not? As she imagined how frenzied the boy would be if no word came from her all night, she got panicky again. The stranger hadn't phoned and it must be getting late. She tried to pray and trust, but the possibility that the young man would merely promise and not bother to go at all began to possess her. At last she could stand it no longer and she rang again for the nurse. But a patient down the hall was in pain and crying out wildly. It was a long time before the nurse returned to Anne. She was a new one and impatient when she did come.

"I thought I told you not to ring unless you had to," she gently scolded.

"Oh please!" begged Anne. "Isn't there *some* way I could get out of here and go home to my brother?"

"Certainly not!" The nurse tried to soothe her. "You

know the doctor said you must lie still or you may be worse. You couldn't go unless he signed a release and we can't call him for that now."

"But it doesn't matter about me," pleaded Anne. "My brother is a little boy and lame. And he's all alone. A young man said he would go and see him but how do I know he went? He promised to call back and he hasn't. Davey will be terrified. He doesn't even know where I am!"

"Well, Miss Wrenn, you will just have to wait till morning."

Then all at once the nurse gave her arm a rub with alcohol and before Anne knew what she was doing she had thrust in a hypodermic needle. In a few minutes Anne dropped into a tortured slumber.

A message came for her but the nurse only wrote it down on a slip to give her later when she would waken. There it lay for half an hour when an interne stopped by the desk and looked for a sheet of paper on which to write a notation. He tore off the scribbled message and laid it underneath the pad while he wrote. Then he continued on his rounds. Along came a nurse, picked up the pad and hurried off with it. An imp of a breeze stole through the open window nearby and, snatching up the unprotected slip of paper, transported it swiftly to a narrow crevice behind the desk where it lay until the night nurse had gone home. The cleaning woman came by later on but she rarely moved that big desk, and although she saw the paper back of the desk and poked at it, it did not follow her broom easily and she gave up and left it lying where it was.

CHAPTER V

AMELIA MATHERS squeezed out her ragged, still-greasy dishcloth and hung it to dry over the edge of the sink. It should have been hung over the towel rack but that would mean several extra steps and Amelia did not feel up to any extra steps this evening. She was a heavy woman, and given to arthritis in her hip. There were times when she dreaded to make a move, lest she stir up afresh the demonlike gnawing pain that never entirely left her. She leaned her weight against the old oilcloth-covered kitchen table as she took off her glasses and wiped them on the bottom of her big, damp, blue-striped apron. A fly chose that moment to rest on her nose and she gave an impatient swoosh to drive it away. Her hand caught in the apron and jerked her glasses in a wide arc to the floor. The right lens broke in a clean, straight line through the center.

Noises of exasperation issued from Amelia's throat, and she groaned in agony as she eased herself down to reach the glasses. Squinting pitifully, she held them off from her and tried to see well enough to match the two pieces together. Fortunately they were not shattered. The two parts fitted without a chip missing. She laid them down and struggled with the heavy wooden kitchen drawer. Rummaging, she drew out a tube of liquid glue. It was going to be difficult with her impaired eyesight to anoint the thin edges of the glass without smearing the lens. She thought of trying to call Harry in to help her, but like as not he would pay no attention, just sit there on the old bench and continue to smoke his pipe. So she hit upon the method of squeezing out a line of glue onto a piece of newspaper. Then feeling along with her fingers to tell just where it was, she pressed the edge of glass into it for a second. To make the two parts meet exactly, and hold them there steadily, required care. The glass would be smeared with the glue on her fingers but it could be cleaned. She stood patiently for several minutes. She dared not move or lay them down, lest she break the adhesion. Finally she felt it was safe to lay them gently on the newspaper to set firmly. Then she took her way across the big kitchen, stepping high across the place where she knew the linoleum was worn and might trip her, and started down the back steps, holding as long as she could to the wooden post supporting the porch roof.

There was a broken board in the second step, she knew that. It had been broken since early spring. She had told Harry to mend it, and scolded him for not mending it, but it still was not mended. She could not see it plainly without her glasses, and besides, it was impossible to see over her large abdomen at any time. She would step wide of the broken place to make sure. There, now she was safe. No! Her foot was not on solid wood. The step gave. She tried to pull back but she was too far off balance. She grabbed for the post again, but it was too late. With a dreadful cry of fright she pitched forward, and an excruciating pain shot through her hip. The bone snapped and her bulky body went down and lay, a pitiful mass, on the ground.

Harry, over on the bench under the maple tree, roused himself to come to her side. He was a small man, with a small chin and small damp hands that seemed to cling to his pipe for support. His apathy was disturbed as it had not been for many a day. He stooped to help his wife to her feet. But she railed at him.

"Let me alone! No! No! Oh-h-h! It's broken! No, you can't help me! Don't try to lift me. It's killing me."

Harry kept on trying, however, but in vain. He couldn't budge her. All the while she moaned and tried to fight him off.

"Get a doctor, can't you?" she screamed. "I've broken my leg, I tell you. I knew this would happen! It's all your fault! I told you months ago to fix—that—step." Her breath came short because of her agony. "Get somebody—to help—I tell you. Dave's gone out. Call Jason."

Harry swore.

"What good would *he* do? He couldn't lift you. Wouldn't if he could!" he finished in a mumble.

The poor woman made an effort to raise herself or shift her position so that Harry could get a purchase on her, but every move only increased her torture. She sank back with another groan.

But she was still the general. She was silent a few moments and then she pantingly gave her commands.

"Harry! Get yourself down the hill to Dawson's and telephone for a doctor and an ambulance. You don't want me to die on your hands, do you. Hurry! Oh-h—Lord! What torment!"

The man started off excitedly.

Suddenly Amelia called him back.

"No, Harry, we can't have an ambulance. We can't afford it. You'll have to get somebody to help me into the house. I can't pay a lot of hospital bills."

But for once Harry put his foot down.

"Yes, you can. You know you can, Amelia. There's all that money you have tied up in those bonds—"

"Be quiet, Harry!" Amelia hushed him furiously in a stage whisper. "Do you want somebody to break into the house? Oh-h-h this pain is killing me. If I die the money won't do me any good. Well, go ahead." She breathed hard. "You'll have to do something for me, quick. What are you waiting for? Get down there and phone!"

After the sound of Harry's footsteps on the gravel had ceased, Amelia tried once more to manipulate her bulk to a sitting posture but she had to give up and then a cold chill seized her. She shook from head to foot and her teeth chattered. She moaned and cried out, but Jason was up on the third floor, nodding over his newspaper, and Dave was on his way back to the city. Nobody came.

It seemed years to her before Harry returned. She had ample time to think. She began by cursing Harry's negligence. Every twinge reminded her of some instance of his procrastination. Then she cursed her brother for keeping up the estrangement between them. If he weren't so pig-headed about Harry he would be on speaking terms with her now and could be of some help. He had always blamed everything on Harry and refused to take his share of the responsibilities because Harry wouldn't take his. It made Harry mad that Jason wouldn't help his own sister so Harry, in turn, had refused to do anything at all. It was all the fault of somebody, the world, or God, or possibly her dead father that the brother and sister were condemned to live in the same house. If her father hadn't given in to her mother's weakness for wanting a house big enough to house both her children and their families, this big omnibus wouldn't have been built in the first place. It should have been sold long ago, and if Jason had managed that offer ten years ago as he should have, it would be off their hands now. They wouldn't be living in a place where the steps were broken and the screens were torn so that they couldn't keep out the flies that came in and sat on people's noses and broke their glasses.

One grievance led to another in the poor woman's tortured mind until she worked herself into a fever and it seemed that she was tossing in a hot cauldron surrounded by a swarm of evil-eyed, ill-natured monsters.

While his aunt was lying at the foot of the back steps in the darkness, Dave was looking after the strangers.

He left the telephone booth with a feeling of frustration. He had been so sure that Darla would be resting at home after her nervous strain, and that his call assuring her of the other girl's welfare would be a welcome relief. Perhaps she was exhausted from the shock of the accident and she had fallen asleep. That must be it. He turned his thoughts back to the little boy he had left.

No doubt the child was at this moment crying himself to sleep. Afraid of the dark like any other child, for all his trust in a God who cared. Dave climbed into his car and started off toward home. But Davey's woebegone expression when he had said good night kept coming before him. He recalled many nights of terror when he was a little boy and his mother had gone off, never to return, she always said. His father had never come to him at such times but had stayed in his own room nursing his grievance, or sought relief down in the city. Little Dave had been left to face his sorrows alone. How much he would have given then for some older brother who would have come in and stayed by him. Just somebody there to talk to! Somebody who cared enough to stay.

Dave drove slowly for six blocks, toward home. Then he made a right turn and a right turn again and headed back toward Pearl Street. He pulled his car up over the low curb to be out of the way of any traffic that might dent his fenders. Then he shut and locked his windows. Up the creaky stairs again. He paused. Yes, it was a little boy's whimpering that he heard. He tapped gently.

"Davey! Davey!" he called under his breath for it was getting late now and others might be asleep. He did not care to face the doughty Mrs. Pincheon tonight.

The whimpering stopped.

"Davey," he said again. "It's Dave. May I come in?"

A muffled cry of joy sounded. "Oh, yes! Come in. Boy, oh boy!"

Davey's arms were outstretched. Awkwardly Dave knelt by the bed and let the boy give him a tight hug. He smoothed the velvet crew cut and a strange warm wave of gladness stole around his heart. It would have been nice to have had a little brother who loved him like this. They could have had great times together. His voice had a gentleness in it that his father or his aunt would have been amazed to hear.

"Kinda dark and lonely, is it, kid?" He switched on a light. Davey gave a little shamed chuckle.

"Kinda," he agreed.

"Would you like me to stay here tonight?"

"Oh boy! *Would*ya?" Davey poked his head up, pointing to the other twin bed. "You could sleep there. Anne wouldn't mind. She's not fussy. She'll be so glad to know somebody's here with me, I know."

Suddenly it came over Dave that he had promised to let that sister know that her Davey was all right.

"Say!" he exclaimed. "I must call the hospital and tell her you are all right. Is there a phone here?"

"No, not in this house, but there's one a couple of blocks down in a drugstore on the corner. It's open till half-past ten. What time is it now?"

"Quarter after. I'll hustle. Be back in a few minutes. Don't be afraid while I'm gone."

"No, I'll be okay. Oh, boy!"

The nurse would not wake her patient so Dave had to leave a message. But he wondered at the sensation he had that all was well. It was a new feeling for him. Mostly things had not been well.

When he reached the room again and considered sleeping on that snowy white chenille bed, he found a deep embarrassment upon him. Gingerly he turned back the spread and lay down on the edge of the covers. He would almost have preferred to sleep on the floor, only Davey would not hear to that.

He wondered how he would manage in the morning without a clean shirt or a razor. This was a crazy thing to do. Why did he let himself in for it? Ever since that accident he had been getting into more and more of a tangle. Tomorrow it would be a good thing to step out of the picture and let all these people get along as best they could. Then he thought of Darla. That poor little girl, with nobody to look out for her, maybe having to go to court all alone and face the barrage of questioning. No, he wouldn't want to desert

Darla, but he certainly owed nothing to these other people, Davey and his sister. He couldn't be expected to look after *both* parties to the accident! In the morning he would stop to see about Darla's car and then call her. From then on he would just have to see how much she needed him. If she showed signs of wanting his friendship, that would make up for the tough time he had had all his life. If not, well, it would be just another disappointment along with the rest. But he could still hear her low voice vibrant in his ear: "You're terrific!" and he thrilled to it again.

Davey was humming a little tune to himself. Every few minutes he would break out with a new attempt at conversation but at last Dave got him hushed up and they both fell asleep.

He stopped at the garage the next morning and found that Darla's car was being taken care of, then he went around by way of the hospital.

It was quite early and they wouldn't let him see Miss Wrenn, but they said she was doing well.

"Did you give her my message?" he asked, feeling frustrated.

"Yes," snapped the sleepy operator, neither knowing nor caring what this early caller was talking about.

He looked at the clock. Seven-ten. Was it too early to call Darla? He dialed her number and let it ring twice. There was no answer, so he hung up quickly. He'd try again later in the day.

He decided that if he drove fast he might be able to make it home before he went to work. Then he could shave and get a clean shirt.

He tore up the hill and into the driveway, avoiding skillfully the gully where the cinders had washed away the shoulder last fall. He parked under the porte-cochere and raced up the stairs.

His father, in the remains of a once-handsome bathrobe, was puttering about the kitchen, glowering.

He blazed out at Dave, "So you have decided to come home, have you? I wouldn't have been surprised if you hadn't come back at all, you know," he added sarcastically, "with the mother you had." He was holding a cup of hot coffee in his trembling hand and he shook so with rage and relief that he could scarcely set it down. "It wouldn't be strange if you never came back. What a place to come to!" He gazed around at the dreary room that he had been staring at through his fears and tears all night while he was struggling between anger and worry.

"Oh, don't blow your stack, Dad," Dave threw back at him. "There's certainly nothing out of the way in spending the night with a—a friend. Keep your shirt on."

But Jason Truscott kept on making incoherent mumblings and glancing toward the bathroom door where Dave was taking a quick shave. A friend! What sort of friend? Not a girl, it was to be hoped! Yet why else Dave's stammering? The father was frantic to know more. He had been in a frenzy lest Dave had been out with a wild crowd, or lest he had been hurt in an accident. He would not for anything let Dave know how much he cared that the boy grow up with decent ideals. It had never occurred to him to try to train him in those ideals.

Dave was sliding into a clean shirt and buttoning it as he ran down the stairs.

"I'll bring some groceries tonight, Dad," he called.

"There's enough left there for your lunch, I think."

He slammed the battered screen door on his way out to his car to smother his father's angry protest.

But out under the porte-cochere, barring the way into the front seat, stood Uncle Harry, trouble written all over his weak, drab countenance.

Uncle Harry rarely figured in Dave's life. Occasionally they had scattered, desultory conversations about the hens, or the new farmhouse going up across the fields, but there had never been any close bond between them. Uncle Harry was on neutral ground, as it were, and if it ever became necessary for communication to be carried on between the Truscott brother and sister it was generally done through Dave and Uncle Harry. Dave despised the pretense of it. If he had anything to say to his aunt he simply went straight to her and said it. But his father nursed old grudges; he was determined to oppose anything they did or thought.

Dave was surprised to find Uncle Harry seeking him out. He did wish that his uncle had chosen some other time to accost him. Without a greeting, Dave waited impatiently to see what he wanted. The old man's discolored eyes were pathetic, like a yellow dog's. His loose wet tobacco-stained lips released his pipe reluctantly when he spoke.

"Your aunt's in the hospital," he stated. He pronounced it "ant" as if his wife were an insect.

"What's the trouble?" barked Dave unfeelingly.

"She fell and broke her hip last night. You were out. Couldn't get a doctor. Had to hire an ambulance to take her to Park Street Hospital."

"That's tough! I'll stop and see her tonight," Dave promised. "Better tell Dad," he motioned toward the upper floor.

Although he knew that the chances were slim that Uncle Harry would tell Dad, it seemed the decent thing to do, as she was his sister.

Dave sighed deeply as he got into the car and started to the factory. More trouble! Now how would the household manage? Uncle Harry was as helpless as a babe. Aunt Amelia had always done everything for him. That was one of the things that made her brother so disgusted.

Dave was not utterly heartless. He had sometimes felt a passing pity for his aunt. But irritation at Uncle Harry's worthlessness and her way of pampering him, always quickly erased any sympathy he had.

Dave was the only hale and hearty one of the menage who could or would take any responsibility for running the household. And he had not the slightest interest in doing so. Let them run themselves into the ground if they cared to. People who were so bull-headed that they couldn't be decently courteous to their own relatives deserved nothing! His thoughts turned to the people he had met yesterday. Their difficulties seemed much more interesting to him, especially Darla's. He would phone her again at his noon hour. That was a bright spot to look forward to in a very gloomy day.

Chapter VI

Darla yawned and stretched. Then she started wide awake. The telephone was ringing. There were always intriguing possibilities in a telephone call. She glanced at the clock. Noon. It might be Merta. She was always hounding her out of bed. She reached for the receiver.

"Yes?" she responded, still sleepy.

An eager masculine voice answered.

"Is that you, Darla?—ah, Miss Dartman?" Dave had a feeling his red face could be seen over the wire. "This is Dave."

"Dave?" Darla's voice was sweet but a little bewildered.

"Yes, Dave Truscott." He paused. "You know. I'm the one who—who helped—who took you to the police station yesterday."

"Oh! Oh, yes!" Darla seemed to be returning from distant dreams. Dave got the impression that she had forgotten that there ever had been any accident, but of course that could not be. She probably just hated to talk about it. Maybe he shouldn't have mentioned the police. It was likely a sore subject with her. He must be more careful. She was such a sensitive little thing.

"I just wanted to let you know that the girl is still alive, and they told me at the hospital that she has nothing worse than cuts and bruises and a broken collarbone. I guess you won't need to worry about heavy lawsuits either, for I talked to her last night a few minutes and she doesn't seem like a person who would try to take advantage of you."

Dave paused. He expected Darla to express relief and thanks, but she was busy trying to light a cigarette. He went on, still eagerly.

"She has a little brother who is a cripple from polio. She was so worried about him staying alone last night that I went over and looked after him. I thought you would have wanted me to do anything possible for them."

"Oh, my word! You really went overboard, didn't you!"

"That's all right, Miss Dartman. I didn't mind a bit. I had nothing special to do last night and it was a pleasure, really. He's a nice little kid. You may like to get acquainted with him. I felt sorry for him. They live in one room and he never gets out. His sister teaches school."

"Well, you certainly did a lot of detective work, didn't you." Was she teasing him? That was probably her way of showing her appreciation. She wasn't the gushy kind who would keep thanking you all over the place.

"I stopped to see about your car, too. It will be ready tomorrow. Have you called your insurance company?"

"Oh, no! I guess I ought to do that, oughtn't I! Oh, I hate to have to go all over the thing!"

"Of course you do!" Dave sympathized. "Why not let me call them? They will come to you eventually with umpteen questions but after a few days it won't seem so terrible to you."

"Oh, would you call them? I'd appreciate that *so* much." Dave couldn't see the curl of Darla's pretty lip and the little assured toss of her head as she flicked the end of her cigarette over the ashtray. This boy was really useful. And he might become more so. Her eyes narrowed.

"Sure, I'll call them. Then they will get in touch with you. It ought to be done right away. They always want to be notified within twenty-four hours, you know."

"Oh, do they? Well, thank you, Dave." Darla managed to put into her words a little more than an ordinary expression of gratitude. At least Dave thought he detected an intimate note in her voice that seemed to place him on a plane with her. He took a deep breath.

All his running around and waiting on strangers was worth it if it would win him friendship with a girl like Darla.

He ventured further.

"I tried to call you last night," he told her, "but I guess you were worn out, weren't you? I didn't ring long, for fear I'd wake you."

"Oh? Oh! Did you call? Really!"

"Yes, and again this morning but I had to make it before I went to work and I guess it was too early for you."

Darla laughed, that slow musical laugh. It sounded especially lovely because she was laughing at herself.

"I was deep in slumber, Dave. I'm sorry!"

Just the way she said "sorry" with a little lingering on the first syllable sent a strange thrill through Dave. It seemed to bring him again a little closer, as if there was some bond of understanding between them. He had never imagined that it could be so wonderful just to talk to a girl over the telephone. It must be that way only when the *right* girl came along!

"Oh, that was all right," he laughed. "I'm glad you could sleep," he added solicitously. "Well," he hesitated, trying to think of some reason to continue the conversation, some further service he might render so that he would have an excuse to call her again, "I'll let you know—ah—ah—I'll stop

in to the hospital again tonight and see how that girl is doing."

Darla smiled complacently to herself.

"Oh, that'll be fine," she agreed. "I'll be home late this
afternoon."

"Okay, then, I'll call. Around five-thirty?"

"That will be fine, Dave." For the third time Dave felt his
head swim with the thrill of her voice as she said "Dave" in
that sweet way she had.

He replaced the receiver, called the insurance company,
and went back to his work in a whirl of joy. He had never
felt like this in all his life. He had a feeling he could do wonders. He worked fast and well. He was figuring how if he
did his best he could soon get ahead in the factory. He would
work hard at night school, too, and perhaps rate a further
raise in pay. There was no limit to what he might do or become with Darla's friendship as an incentive. He would be
talking to her again today. He must remember to stop at the
hospital to see that other girl on the way home from work.

The thought of the hospital and the pale, sweet-faced girl
there who had been so troubled the night before, reminded
him of Davey. He wondered how he was getting on. It must
seem a long time to the child between mornings and evenings when his sister returned. He would like to take him
something tonight. Dave's heart was warm with joy and it
wanted some expression. Perhaps he could find a little air-
plane model for Davey to put together. This was pay day,
fortunately, or he wouldn't be able to buy anything, even
dinner tonight. He knew he couldn't buy anything for Darla
yet, not till he knew her better. A nice girl would resent it.
But if he could get something for the little boy it would be
sort of like giving it to Darla.

So he stopped at a dime store on his way to see Anne and

found a little helicopter model, something like those he had described to Davey the night before when he told him about the factory. It was the first time in his life that Dave had bought a present for a little boy and he was amazed at the warm eagerness he felt. He had had no idea there could be such pleasure in giving.

All day long, underneath the current of his dreams about Darla, the ugly monster of his responsibility toward Aunt Amelia had been lying in wait. Dave could not picture himself looking after a bedridden, nagging old woman, let alone her lazy husband. Aunt Amelia would simply have to cough up and hire somebody to look after her, at least part time.

He went to Anne's hospital first as it was first on his way. He was feeling rather pleased with himself that he was doing so much beyond what would be reasonably expected of him. Anne would no doubt be delighted to see him since he had been with her brother. Very likely she would have made some provision for a friend to stay with Davey by this time, but it might cheer her to find how brave Davey had been last night about the whole thing.

But when he tapped and entered the room at the nurse's response he met a pair of very cold brown eyes.

He tried to smile pleasantly.

"How are you today, Miss Wrenn?"

Anne looked squarely at him and looked away, barely murmuring, "All right, thank you." She closed her eyes as if she was too tired and too troubled to bother with him.

Dave glanced over at the nurse. She was not the one he had seen first and spoken to on the phone the evening before. She looked at him questioningly as if to say, "What right have you here? Are you a friend or a relative?"

Dave felt squelched. This was a fine reception for one

who had gone out of his way to do a favor, and had even given up his own bed to keep a strange boy company. He had expected warm thanks even to effusiveness, for he knew very well that what he had done was far more than most people would have bothered to do. He felt like echoing his father's favorite remark, "That's thanks for you! Dogs are more grateful than humans."

Dave stood a moment, uncertain what to do or say. The nurse was looking toward her patient as if to get her cue from the way Miss Wrenn would receive him. She wasn't quite sure whether the girl knew him so well that she did not feel called upon to be polite or whether she did not care to see the gentleman. She was feverish. Perhaps the caller would make her worse.

Finally Dave said, "I just wondered whether there was any message you would like me to take to Davey."

Anne turned and looked at him with open scorn.

"No, *thank* you! There is no need for you to bother at all about him."

She might as well have slapped him. Her tone stung like the lash of a strap.

He started to retort but remembered in time that she was sick. You couldn't depend on what sick people did. But she didn't look like a delirious patient. He couldn't understand it. The corners of the little package in his pocket pressed against his arm as if to remind him of his next errand. Why bother, if she was going to act like that? His temper flared. He had spent one of his hard-earned dollars to get something he thought the boy would like, and now this!

He hesitated, anger in his face, and fingered the package. What he would like to have done was throw it in her face. But she was a girl, and sick. That wouldn't do. He had no other use for the toy. He was not acquainted with any other little boys who might like it. He still felt warmly toward the child. Let him have it, but *he* wouldn't take it to him. He tossed it down on the foot of the bed.

"Okay, Miss Wrenn, if that's the way you feel about it. I bought this for him, but you can give it to him some other time." He spoke with obviously suppressed anger and Anne glanced up at him again, with surprise and weariness in her eyes.

"I suppose you are trying hard to make an impression," she said caustically, "so that I won't bring suit. Don't bother. I have no intention of doing so."

Dave stood and looked down at her, angry and silent. Finally he spoke with restraint.

"Now look here, Miss Wrenn, I don't know what you are driving at. If I had realized that you didn't really want me to go out to Davey last night I certainly wouldn't have gone. I felt sorry for the youngster and I saw you were in a jam. But evidently you are angry that I presumed to stay there. You would rather have me out of the picture. I shall gladly step out. Good-bye."

The nurse looked relieved but Anne looked aghast. And the discarded package lay unnoticed on the foot of the bed, while Dave marched angrily down the long corridor to the elevator.

Chapter VII

Anne had spent a miserable day after a tortured night. The pain of her bruises had begun to wear on her, but far greater than that was the anxiety over Davey. She could picture his bed all awry; dirty dishes; maybe no food left; no water for washing; and no massage for his legs. All night long she had imagined she heard him crying for her. Did he know where she was? Had the young man gone to him or not with her message? Over and over she tried to think what had probably happened, but she was in a turmoil when morning dawned and she still had no word. For the little slip of paper was still lying on the floor behind the desk.

Her night nurse had thought her merely feverish, but the one who came on next morning was more sympathetic. Anne finally persuaded her to call one of her teacher friends and ask her to go to Davey before school. The nurse came back with the assurance that the girl would be glad to do it and Anne was somewhat relieved. But she spent all the morning and afternoon building up resentment toward the young man who had promised so blandly to go and then never went near the boy. She kept thinking of all the scornful phrases she would like to use to him.

It was time she learned not to trust *any*body—but God. There, that was her trouble. She had known it all along but wouldn't face it. She wasn't trusting God to look after Davey. She had tried to worry over him herself all night. What a fool she had been. In her heart she cried out for forgiveness and a measure of peace came. But when Dave appeared suddenly she was taken unawares and the resentment flared up. All the bitter accusations she had thought of during those hours in the night came back to her. It was all she could do to hold her tongue. She had no idea how her icy tone cut.

But when Dave froze up and walked out of the room she suddenly came to herself. The little plane in its brown-paper wrapping lay accusingly at the foot of her bed to plead for him. If he had heartlessly ignored him, why would he have bought it? He spoke as if he had gone to see Davey last night. Was it possible he was telling the truth? Perhaps she had all the wrong slant on the matter.

In panic she called the nurse as she was going out the door.

"Go after him, please, and make him come back! I want to talk to him."

"You'd do better to let him go, Miss Wrenn. He has upset you and you already have a fever."

"No! *Please* get him. I'll be worse if you don't. Please. Go quickly before he gets away."

The nurse hesitated. This pale, sweet-faced girl was turning out to be a difficult patient. When she saw the frenzy the girl was working herself into, she hurried down the long hall after Dave.

She caught him as he was about to step into the elevator.

"Miss Wrenn would like you to come back, sir," she spoke sternly.

Dave paused, uncertain. Indignation still hardened his face.

The elevator operator showed impatience. He started to enter and then stepped back. After all, the girl was sick. If she wanted to apologize he might as well give her a chance.

Finally, with his head held high he followed the nurse's stiff back down the long hallway.

Anne's face held a mixture of animosity and humiliation. For a moment they remained silent, fixing each other with hostile gaze.

Anne spoke first.

"I want to apologize," she said, struggling to speak meekly, "for the way I acted just now. I had no right to question your sincerity. I have been desperate all night and all day to hear some word of Davey, and I took it out on you. I realize that we have no claim on you whatever. There was no reason for you to go to see Davey. I should not blame you. I hope you will pardon my rudeness." She had begun humbly, but she stiffened up considerably before she finished her little speech. Her cheeks were flushed with fever and her brown eyes that looked so steadily at him were beautiful with earnestness.

Dave couldn't help admiring her. He had never been taught to apologize for such things himself and he could only stand awkwardly silent. He did not even know how to accept an apology graciously.

Finally he stammered out, "Oh, that's all right. Forget it. I—I just took a liking to the kid and thought he'd enjoy a new toy. I promised him I'd come back, but if you don't want me to—" Again his hurt pride asserted itself and he left the sentence unfinished.

Anne stared at him. She had persuaded herself so thoroughly that he had not gone to see Davey, that she could not adjust herself now to believing that he had.

"You mean you really did go last night, after all?"

"Certainly I did," he retorted in a chilly tone. "I believe I told you I would go."

"Yes, you did," assented Anne meekly. "But," she added

with the first hint of a twinkle in her eye, "you must remember that I don't know you from Adam, and when I didn't hear anything, I took for granted that you were just in league with the nurse, trying to calm me down."

Dave's eyebrows lifted a trifle disdainfully. Then he suddenly realized that what she had said was true and he laughed. The temperature rose considerably between them.

"You must have had somewhat the same experience with people as I have," he said with bitterness. " 'Don't trust nobody nohow,' I say!"

She gave a weak laugh and a keen glance, then she looked away lest he catch her studying him. What had happened in his life to make him feel so distrustful of everybody in general? He was such a nice-looking boy, and he looked so straightforward himself, why was he so bitterly disillusioned? Her heart relented just a degree toward him. After all, she had been feeling just the same way a few minutes ago. There wasn't anybody but God to trust, when all was said and done. She wondered if this proud sensitive boy knew God well enough to trust Him.

"I guess you're about right," she agreed sympathetically, "—almost!"

He caught her eyes and held them.

"What do you mean 'almost'?" he growled.

"I mean you can always count on God, that is, if you are His child. The only trouble is, I forget to, sometimes."

Dave shrugged, started to argue and then remembered that she was a feverish patient and held his peace. His shrug told her a great deal, however, and her heart went out to him.

"Well, if you will forgive me, please, I would like to thank you for visiting Davey last night."

"It's okay. Forget it." He waved his hand carelessly. He

had had enough of the matter. Better let it drop and let him drop out of the picture. How could he get away quickly? He was eager to call Darla.

"Would you mind telling me how he was?" Anne asked in an eager, submissive little voice.

The question took Dave back to the tiny room and somehow he seemed to feel those boyish arms around him again. The flavor of the boy's ready love was sweet to him. He smiled.

"He was a little soldier, all right," he told her. "He was crying 'a little,' he said, before I came, but he was okay after that. We had a good time. It was all I could do to stop him talking so we could get to sleep."

"Sleep!" cried Anne. "You don't mean you stayed all night with him!"

"Sure," replied Dave casually. "Didn't you get my message? I sent word I was going to stay. Davey said you wouldn't mind." Dave was watching her sharply again. Had she taken offense because she felt he had presumed in spending the night in her room with her brother?

But all he saw was utmost mortification. Her eyes seemed to grow larger and tears stood in them.

"You did that, a perfect stranger, and I treated you the way I did! No wonder you were angry. Oh, can you ever forgive me? I didn't know."

Dave was embarrassed now. If only he could get out of here! He didn't know what to do when a woman cried.

"It's okay, I tell you. Forget it. I enjoyed it."

"Oh, but I'm so ashamed. No, they didn't give me your message. The nurse who was on then has been transferred. How can I ever thank you?"

"Skip it!" ordered Dave. He felt better now, being on the

benevolent end of things. He could afford to be gracious.

"I can't!" persisted Anne. "I'll never forgive myself." She tried to reach for the little plane. "Would you prove that you forgive me by taking this to him as you planned?" she asked wistfully.

Dave hesitated. It was getting late. He ought to have called Darla by now. He was anxious to get away. But perhaps the quickest way to make a getaway would be to take the package and go. It wouldn't be too far out of his way. He would call Darla first.

"Okay," he agreed. "Sure, I'll take it. And don't worry if they don't give you any message tonight. But I'll try to call you if I can. Good night. Hope you are soon better."

He was edging out the door, anxious to leave before further conversation got started.

"Here!" called Anne. "Here is money to get some supper and groceries for him. Yes, please. I insist!" she urged when he would have waved her off.

He took the money, noted what Anne told him to buy, and was off.

He did not wait until he was out of the hospital to phone. Even now it was ten minutes past the time Darla had told him to call. Maybe she would be offended. Maybe she was going out. He dialed nervously.

No answer. Maybe he had dialed incorrectly. He tried again. Still no answer. In unhappy frustration he blamed Anne for making him lose the chance to talk to Darla. She had said five-thirty. It was nearly quarter of six now. She had probably gone out for dinner. She would think he hadn't cared to call.

Disappointment settled dismally upon him. He turned away from the booth feeling very much alone. How strange

that he could have learned already to count on a companion-
ship with an almost total stranger, just on the strength of
two conversations. It gave him a wonderful lift to talk to
Darla. He lived in the pleasure of it until the next call. He
wondered whether she was a little bit disappointed that he
had not called. But that was more than he could hope for.
She had seemed to like him, but of course she couldn't be
expected to care as much as he did. He had no illusions
about his own charm. Still, he kept hearing her voice and
seeing her big blue eyes raised to his as she said, "You're
terrific!" when he took her home that first night. That moment had seemed to change everything for Dave. No one
had ever said that to him before. Since then he had walked
with a new assurance and held his head erect instead of
slumping into his usual discouraged droop.

Well, the next thing was to get some groceries before the
stores closed. Then he would run over to Davey's room and
take him the plane. He would talk a few minutes, stop at
Aunt Amelia's hospital and then go home. Dad would be
raging for his dinner. Dave sighed. Why was it that the nice
things were always eluding him, and the ugly unpleasant
things were always thrusting themselves into his path?

He wound the crowded narrow streets again and parked
once more with his car part-way up on the low curbing lest
in the straitened passage of Pearl Street his fenders get battered.

He started up the unvarnished, squeaky stairs, worn hol-
low and splintery by the shuffling of many roomers through
the years. A man was at the head of the flight, about to come
down. He appeared to be about forty. He wore a natty
striped suit, trim-fitting around the hips as if he were proud
of his figure. His straight, black hair, greased flat, was cut

low in front of his ears. "Cheap!" noted Dave to himself as he passed him. "It must be the man Davey's sister doesn't trust. I don't blame her."

The man stared at Dave at the top of the stairs. He raised his eyebrows and curled his lip in surprise when Dave knocked at the door at the end of the hall. Then he shrugged and went down.

Davey greeted his new friend with a whoop and a hug. His warm guileless eagerness helped to soothe Dave's fretted spirit.

Davey wanted to put the little plane together without delay and Dave, boylike, hung over him and directed him. It was an intricate little model and the time passed quickly.

Davey's pleasure in the toy was something entirely new to Dave. He had not been around children for some years and he did not remember much that was joyful in his own childhood. He was amazed at the clean, light feeling it gave him to watch Davey enjoy his gift.

The boy was considerably upset, however, to find his sister was not to come right home. He sighed deeply, and the tears almost got the better of him. He struggled to swallow them down and give a brave smile at Dave.

"Will you come and stay with me?" he managed at last. He had perfect confidence that Dave enjoyed their time together as much as he did.

Dave started to shake his head decidedly no. Then he paused to consider. If he took enough groceries home for two or three days his father could get along perfectly well. It would save gas if he didn't have to keep going back and forth. He would be right on the spot to do anything for Darla in case the need arose. Why not? There was the gratifying sense that he was doing a very good deed. He would be expected to squeeze in a visit to Aunt Amelia occasionally, too. Yes, it would certainly be more convenient if he were in town.

Davey saw that he had gained a foothold, and he coaxed. Finally Dave agreed to go home and see how things were and come back if it were possible. It occurred to him that life might be much pleasanter if he could ditch the whole menage at home and get a room in the city. Then he'd be free to do little kindly acts like staying with this boy, for instance. Why was it that a kindness for a stranger was so much more fascinating than the thousand and one kindnesses that he might do for his own relatives?

He stopped at the little dingy drugstore to try Darla's phone again, but there was still no answer. The deflated feeling that came every time he failed to get her was annoying.

With irritation he started on the other errand that must be accomplished before he went home, the call on Aunt Amelia. He wondered how it was that he had suddenly got himself involved with so many dependents all at once. He would have to shake some of them soon. He couldn't keep this up. This was like a doctor's life, or a country preacher's. Tomorrow there would be his night-school class in engineering. He wouldn't have time to make calls.

Next door to the hospital where they had taken Aunt Amelia was a florist's shop. He paused. In the window was a breath-taking arrangement of pale pink roses and delphinium. They reminded Dave of Darla's blue eyes and the soft petal-like coloring of her cheeks. How he would like to send her a box of those! He stayed several minutes drinking them in. Her face seemed to appear and smile at him right in the middle of the flowers. He could hear her exclamation at their loveliness, and her low musical laugh. She seemed to smile just for him and say again, "You're terrific, Dave!" lingering on his name in that caressing way. He took a deep breath. This was pay day. He could. But would she resent it? From her point of view he scarcely knew her, although he felt as if he had always known her, longer than either of them had lived. No, he was balmy, this would never do. He sighed and tore himself away, grimly preparing his mind to face Aunt Amelia.

Amelia Mathers was fighting her way through miles of flame and burning thirst. She had no idea how many miles there were to go. Time and again she had sought a way out, but no matter which way she turned the fires were there, hotter than ever. She couldn't even lie down and let them burn her to ashes. Something drove her on. People spoke to her, giving her commands, pretending to soothe her, promising it would be better soon, but they gave her no relief. On she plodded, terribly aware of the torturing flames that seemed to focus on her right leg and make it impossible to progress.

She was not sure who had started the fire. Sometimes she had the impression that it was her brother Jason who had done it. But when in her delirium she accused him of it he always denied any responsibility in the matter and blamed it on her husband's carelessness and neglect. It probably was Harry's fault.

Dave wasn't there. She kept calling for him. He was the only one with a grain of human kindness, or any sense to know what a person needed. He might be able to put out the fire if he would only come. But he didn't care. She knew that. There was no reason why he should; only the natural tie of blood. That didn't seem to count any more. Look at

Jason. It was Jason's fault that the boy didn't care. He had poisoned his mind. But what did it all matter now? This flame was the only thing that mattered. Would nobody ever put it out and cool off her leg?

Harry was calling her. She tried to answer, but the flames choked her voice. She wanted very much to speak to him, but she couldn't. She wanted to settle the blame securely on him for what had happened. And also she wanted to remind him that the social security check would be in next week, and that he was to live on what there was until then. She was determined not to cash any of those bonds. They must be kept for their old age when they might need them more than they did now. That horror was always before her. They might be penniless some day! Who would look after them? Not Jason. Dave couldn't, or wouldn't. Who else was there? Her minister and the people she knew at the church she attended so regularly must not know, no, not if she were ever so hard up. It would be a disgrace! They wouldn't help anyway. They might talk around among themselves, and have it announced, perhaps, in the morning service, that the poor Mathers were destitute and that a purse should be taken up to present to them. Or perhaps they would suggest that old clothes and groceries be sent them. She knew how they would do it. And she could imagine all the gossip and sharp criticism that would accompany any such appeals. She did not care to be on the receiving end of that kind of charity. No, they *must not* touch the bonds.

Harry stopped calling her. He must have gone away. She heard a woman's voice and a woman's gentle hand cool on her brow. That was good. But then the woman said she was going to give her something to make her feel better. She seemed to enter a place then where even the flames were not bright any more, but dark, and she was less able to fight them. She sank in exhaustion, ready to give up.

She thought she heard Dave call her but she couldn't see him. Dave spoke gently, almost as if he cared. That helped a lot but she couldn't tell him so.

The flames burned on. This must surely be Hell. How was it that she had arrived here when she had been such a good member of the church? Her pastor had always assured his people that faithful church attendance would be insurance for eternity. It must be that her record had been lost. She started searching for it, but her glasses were broken and she had difficulty seeing her way. Anyway, if it were anywhere there, the flames would have burned it up long ago. What hope was there for her? She moaned in despair.

Dave stood looking down at his aunt with pity. He had not expected to find her so helpless. She had always been what he called a "female dreadnought," staving ahead, doing more than her share of the necessary work because her husband never got to it and they had to eat. Here she was with her thin hair pulled back into puny pigtails, her pitiful old face shrunken and her lips sagging in, for the nurse had taken out her false teeth. Her leg was strung up in a cast in the air with pulleys and weights on it. She kept tossing and moaning in her fever and delirium. What an end to come to, if it was the end. Dave was ashamed of a momentary relief at the thought, for that would mean one less person to do the grumbling at home. But how much worse would be his own predicament with two old men on his hands! His father was not as old as Uncle Harry, but he was decrepit. What a mess. What had he ever done or not done that he deserved to be tangled up in it all? And now he had taken on several strangers as well to look after. He must be a top-quality sucker!

He did not stay when he saw that Aunt Amelia did not know him. He had a word with the interne and the nurse, learning enough to report to Uncle Harry and his dad.

Downstairs he stopped at the hospital phone booth and tried to call Darla again. His face grew red and his hands fumbled in eagerness as he dialed. Again no answer. Thoroughly discouraged, he started home.

Chapter VIII

The sunset colors had faded when Dave reached the desolate house on the hill. Futile gusts of wind were plucking at the dreary weather-beaten shutters, and pulling on the dingy old curtains that looked more like ragged dusters than curtains.

The sky was overcast. Only one angry red spot remained in the west. Discouragement seemed to swathe the old place and lean down and wrap Dave up in it as he approached.

What was the use in going home? It was worse each time. His night of sleeping in that tiny room on the edge of a strange bed with a helpless little boy to take care of seemed delightful compared to this. He wondered again what made the difference, what was the secret of it? Was it simply that he did not know the sordidness of the strangers' lives yet? When he did, would they seem as dull and abhorrent as his own? Yet there couldn't be very much that he had missed in that tiny place. Its daily routine was turned inside out for him to see even in the short time he had spent there. It was pitiful, but there was a warmth there that was lacking in his own home. He finally decided that it was the boy's loving greeting and his eager arms outstretched that made the difference. What would it be to come home to his father's smile and loving welcome? Dave could not imagine such a thing. And as for a cheery welcome from either his aunt or uncle, he had never heard one in all his life. Nothing but wrangling and fretting. He decided that if he ever had a home of his own he would smile at his children no matter if there wasn't a crust of bread to give them. The bitterness deepened against his own people who had failed to make home a bright place for his childhood.

He trudged up the steep back stairs. Resentment, fostered by his father, flared against Aunt Amelia because she had consigned them to the third floor back. As if his father didn't own half of the house! It was Jason Truscott's pride that wouldn't allow him to unbend enough to argue the point with his sister and demand his share. Dave had tried several times to get the situation straightened out but each party was adamant and he finally gave up.

His father was seated by the window in the gathering gloom. He had not made any attempt to clear away the dishes left from his noon meal, nor to start anything in the way of preparation for supper, although it was now long past mealtime.

Dave's indignation increased but he said nothing, just stood and glared at his father a moment and stalked into the kitchen.

He slammed things around considerably in his irritation and when in a few minutes he had some food ready he did not bother to take off his father's dirty dishes. He merely shoved them aside angrily and set the fresh food at his place.

He glanced over at his father who sat still, watching his movements with bitterness. He could not bring himself to say pleasantly, "Supper's ready, Dad," although he knew that was what he should do, and he would have given a lot to be able to say it. The words and gracious manner simply were not in him.

He sat down to his own meal. All right, if his father wanted to be grumpy let him eat a cold supper alone.

As Dave took the first mouthful suddenly the scene

changed and he seemed to see the velvet head of a little boy bowed reverently expressing his earnest thanks for the food which he had not been able to get himself. For the first time in his life it occurred to Dave that perhaps there was something due a God who had provided, even so sparsely, for him and his father. He had a strange desire to stop and at least recognize the Power who had made it possible to go on and not starve. But he shook off the feeling. He certainly couldn't bow his head here in front of his father. He could imagine the cold cackle of a laugh his father would give if he should try it. He still smarted from various times in his youth when moments of sentiment had been stung to death with scorn.

After a minute his father rose painstakingly and shuffled across and took his seat. The older man ate a while in silence because he couldn't think of words that would sufficiently express his biting fury. At last he burst forth.

"Late again!" He glared across at Dave. "I suppose there was another accident?" he suggested caustically. His shiny eyes were black with malice.

Dave dragged his thoughts along to follow his father's remark. So much had occurred since the evening before that he had forgotten that he had been late yesterday.

"Oh! Why, yes, as a matter of fact, there was. Last night's accident right here." He spoke accusingly. "I had to stop and see Aunt Amelia in the hospital."

"Hospital!" barked his father. "What's she there for?"

"You mean Uncle Harry didn't tell you? I suggested this morning that he let you know."

Jason Truscott made an incomprehensible noise of disgust.

"His royal highness has been out under the maple tree

smoking his pipe most of the day. He was too much occupied, I suppose, with the affairs of state—his own state of slothfulness!" Jason swore harshly. "Well, what happened?" he snapped.

"She fell on the back steps last night and broke her hip."

"I've known that would happen. Serves them right," Jason burst out. Dave said nothing. He knew it did serve them right, but that didn't help matters.

Jason glowered awhile and Dave finished his supper. While Dave took the dishes out to the improvised sink, his father sat still with his head in his hands. Maybe Dad did care. Surely he must remember something pleasant about his sister from childhood days. But at last Jason broke out with:

"Well, what are we expected to do about it?"

Just like him, thought Dave. Hardhearted. Never a thought for his poor old sister.

"I wouldn't know," responded Dave sourly.

Jason gave forth with a drawn out sound of "a" as in cat, which his son had always understood to mean utter disgust and said, "Let the lazy old man she married take care of her. Do him good to have something he has to do. She'll grumble enough till he does it, too!" Jason gave an ugly laugh.

Dave shook his head.

"I'd hate to have him nurse me!" he said with heat.

His father laughed again, finishing with a snort of disdain.

"I'd take poison first," he said, and thought he meant it.

Dave went into his bedroom and gathered some clothes together. He had no suitcase. He had never taken any trips since he could remember. He rummaged and found a suitbox in a closet. He dumped out onto the closet shelf the old clothes that were in it and laid his own in, tying it neatly with string.

"I won't be home for a day or two, Dad." He tried to make his voice sound casual. "I'm staying in town with a friend who is all alone and sick. I thought, seeing as I'll have to be visiting Aunt Amelia every day, I might as well not waste the gas to go back and forth so much. Tomorrow night is school night, anyway. I brought enough groceries to last till I get back."

His father was speechless. Dave walked down the stairs and out of the building before he could say anything.

Then he shook his cane after the boy with a trembling hand.

"A friend that's alone, eh! And sick! eh? What is your own father, I'd like to know? A-a-ah!" Again that ugly short "a" sound that was almost like an animal's snarl.

Disappointment and frustration took hold of the old man till he began to feel that warning surge of blood in his head and knew that he should calm down. No use having another spell now, not with two or three days of solitude to live through.

But Dave felt freer than he had in a long time. He actually had a kindly feeling in his heart for Uncle Harry as he stopped at the kitchen door to tell him how Aunt Amelia was. He did take a rather gruesome delight in making the details of her illness as startling as he could, hoping to scare the old nincompoop into showing some concern for her. All the man did was look blank and helpless.

"How long do they think she will be there?" he asked hopelessly.

"I didn't even ask. It will be a wonder if she pulls through at all," added Dave cruelly.

The man groaned. "I don't know how I'm going to get along here," he mourned.

Dave gave a glance at the sink piled with dishes, and the floor that had not been swept since Aunt Amelia swept it. With disgust he turned on his uncle.

"Listen, Uncle Harry," he warned. "I think it's time you stopped thinking so much about yourself and considered other people's troubles a little. If you had taken a little pains for Aunt Amelia and kept things mended and in order around here this might not have happened."

Uncle Harry took his pipe slowly out of his mouth, stirred up as much as he ever was over anything.

"Look here, you young rascal," he retorted, "I've never seen *you* do anything much yerself around here. You don't put yerself out of yer way none to help yer aunt and you're not the one to talk to me. Mind your own affairs. If I wasn't considerate enough of your pauper father to let him live here, where would you both be, I'd like to know? Been living here on charity these years and then think you can turn on the hand that's been willin' ta help you! You can keep yer mouth shut or be turned out. I'm tellin' ya."

While he spoke Dave grew fiery red and then the blood left his face. His fists knotted and he held them to his sides with an effort.

"Harry Mathers," he spoke in a strained voice between his teeth, "you are lying and you know it. My father has just as much right here in this house as Aunt Amelia. It belonged to their father and he left it to them both. *You* have no right nor part in it. What have you ever done to help keep it up? What have you ever done for anybody in the world, you stinker! You yellow cur!" He took a threatening step toward his uncle who cowered and stepped back behind the refrigerator. "I've never said this to you before for Aunt Amelia's sake, but she's not here now, and if she doesn't come back don't think *you* are going to enjoy what was hers. *You* can get out. The sooner the better, in my opinion. I'm not joking. I'll see that you do!"

He strode down the rickety steps and flung himself into the car and drove off furiously.

Uncle Harry forgot to replace his pipe for the moment in his fright. He peered out from his hiding place until the car was out of the yard. Then he stood at the kitchen door and satisfied himself by making a leering grimace after his bold, broad-shouldered nephew from a safe distance.

Back went his pipe between his wet, loose lips and yellow teeth again as he muttered, "Never did think any good would come of that boy. Worthless just like his dad. No use trying to help such." He made his way back to the couch to rest. Rain had settled into a drizzle. He always took cold if he got wet. He couldn't go out tonight in it. In the morning he would take a bus and go to town himself to see whether Amelia was as bad as Dave said. Likely the boy was making out she was worse than she really was, just to be mean to him.

Dave had intended to stop at the nearest drugstore to try to phone Darla again, but there was no parking space there so he went on to the next. By that time he was so near to Rock Creek Park that he thought it wouldn't do any harm just to drive by the apartment house. He always enjoyed a drive through the park, even in the rain. He took great pleasure in the fact that the lovely girl he had met lived in such a lovely place.

He drove slowly, gazing with one eye up at the windows of the apartment house that overlooked the park. He wondered idly which one was hers. All at once he realized that he was drawing too close to the car in front of him. It had slowed down noticeably and was about to turn in at the driveway to a basement garage. Then he recognized the driver. It was Darla. She must have borrowed a car from the garage until hers should be fixed.

Impulsively, Dave tooted his horn gently. Darla glanced back in her mirror and he waved his hand. She pulled up at the curb and he slowed down beside her. This was a break he hadn't expected.

He opened his right window and leaned across in spite of the rain. He was not aware of the shine in his handsome dark eyes, nor of the attractive way he had of smiling. His teeth were white and even and he had a wide smile, guileless and disarming.

She smiled a welcome.

All of a sudden Dave was embarrassed. He had thought it so imperative that he call Darla, but now he couldn't recall what it was that he ought to say to her. Nothing seemed important except that he was looking at her again. He grew red and stammered eagerly, "Hiyah. How are you?" almost as if she had been very sick for some time and had just begun to convalesce.

Her etched brows went up a little amusedly, but in the dim light he could not see them. She answered, "Just fine, thank you."

"I—I've been trying to get you on the phone," he told her importantly.

"You have?" She appeared to be surprised.

"Yes. Do you work somewhere?"

"Why no, not exactly."

"Did you have something to tell me?" asked the girl gently. "Why don't you park over there and come on upstairs? It's number 11-0-2. I'm afraid we're blocking traffic here."

"Oh!" Dave glanced around. It hadn't occurred to him that there was anybody else on the road. "Oh!" he said again. "All right, I'll be glad to. Just for a minute, you know. I'll have to be getting on." He sought a parking space while Darla proceeded into the garage.

He took the front steps at a gallop. It was like him not to snatch for a guise of dignity as some might have done on entering the exclusive, ultra-modern atmosphere of the building that was Darla's home. He disliked pretense. He was pleased and eager and he didn't care who knew it.

In the elevator he swallowed hard several times. This was the most exciting thing that had happened to him. He had never dared to hope that he would be invited up to visit her. He wondered what her folks would be like. He gave an inward shudder when he thought of his own home in comparison with this. He touched the bell, imagining Darla's smile as she would appear at the door in answer to his ring.

She looked just as bewitching as she always did, dimpling her welcome. Dave had a feeling that there were several other people in the room but he soon discovered that the impression came from their own movements reflected in the myriad mirrors lining the walls. There were no pictures, but everywhere he looked he saw Darla from a different angle. It was fascinating.

Darla was dressed all in black today with a gold belt, and she looked like a fashion figure in a shop window. She curled gracefully into her chaise longue after indicating a straighter chair for him nearby. She could have preceded him by only a few moments but she had already prepared two tall cold drinks on a stand by the couch. Giving him one, she lightly touched his glass with hers and smiled again. He sipped it and he thought nothing had ever tasted so delicious.

"Did you have something to tell me?" asked Darla again sweetly as she sipped her drink.

"Oh, why, yes." Dave had done a little recollecting in the elevator. "I went to see that girl again last night. I don't think she's going to give you any trouble. At least she said she wasn't." He felt rather silly now, telling Darla that; as if she had known it all the time and it was a small thing to her. It had seemed very important before. He tried to add more to make it seem worth his visit.

"I had promised her I would go out to see her brother, you know," he went on, describing events in detail. "Davey's a cute youngster. You might like to go and see him sometime. We could take him for a ride. These spring days—" Dave's voice trailed off for his words seemed to be more and more unnecessary. Darla was laughing at him.

"You are quite the philanthropist, aren't you?" she teased. He reddened.

"Oh no," he shook his head, grinning and embarrassed. "I just—oh, I don't know. I couldn't help thinking how tough it must be to lie there every day all alone. You know, I've often thought . . ." he set down his glass and paused, letting his gaze wander to a dark corner of the room where a white alabaster nymph poised on one toe as if reaching for something, "I've often thought I'd like to hunt up kids like that that are so lonely and helpless and try to make up for a little of the unfairness of—everything." He finished awkwardly, lamely. He felt as if he hadn't made Darla understand the strong urge within him, the terrible need to fight the inevitable weight of sorrow in the world.

But Darla stared in amused silence a moment and then turned back to her glass.

"Tall, tanned and—" she shook her head as if he were hopeless—"adolescent." She finished with a sophisticated little smile, half teasing and half flattering.

Red flamed up in Dave's face. He squirmed uncomfortably. What did she mean? Was she making fun of him? His eyes glared hesitatingly. She saw his uncertainty and laughed, laying a soft little jeweled hand on his knee placatingly.

"You're not hurt?" she purred. "You will have to get used to my teasing." Her dimple showed again and she underscored it with a smile that capsized Dave's heart all over again. Once more she was the angel, he the slave. She was obviously leaving her hand on his knee on purpose. She laughed provocatively. He reached for it awkwardly and gave it a boyish squeeze. He didn't think she would like it if he stroked it as he wanted to do. It was too soon. He released it quickly and she laughed again. He reddened, more confused than ever.

"You're terrific!" she told him once more. His heart pounded. All he wanted to do was sit and look at her.

"Tell me more about yourself," she demanded. "Where do you work?"

He stammered an answer. Skillfully she drew him on to talk of himself. She showed great interest in the research plant.

"Oh, Davey!" she exclaimed. "Do they ever let visitors go through? *Would* you take me some time? I just adore seeing how they make things." She had put on her little-girl look and she was irresistible.

"Why, sure! I'd love to. When do you want to go? I don't think visitors are allowed in the lab itself, but they may let them into the helicopter plant."

"When is it open?" Darla asked eagerly.

"They work in shifts. The place never closes, I guess."

Dave's head was fairly swimming with wonder. She was practically asking for a date. He could see the fellows staring already. He wasn't at all sure that he would be allowed to bring her but he could try. He wasn't going to take the chance of losing a date with Darla by hesitating. Better say yes and find out later if he couldn't. He could take her somewhere else if necessary. It might take his entire pay for the week but it was worth it.

"I have a date tonight," she said. "How about tomorrow? Pick me up here at seven. Then you can take me out to dinner afterward." She smiled graciously.

Something seemed to wrench at Dave's heart an instant. Tomorrow night! Thursday. School night!

"I—I'd love to," he pleaded earnestly, "but— I have a night-school class tomorrow."

Darla's eyebrows raised and she shrugged one shoulder. "Oh, all right." She tossed her chin the least bit. "Don't put yourself out. I thought you asked me to set a time. Far be it from me to insist on a date."

"Oh, please!" begged Dave. "Don't get the idea I don't want to take you. I'd rather do that than—anything in the world."

The pretty eyebrows arched again in a smile. "Really? It didn't sound like it." She was pouting now and she did look sweet.

"But I would!" protested Dave. "Truly I would. Only—"

"You would, *'only!'*" she teased. "Only there's something you'd rather do." She gave another taunting little smile.

"No, honestly, Darla. I'll prove it to you. I'll—I'll *skip* school. There! Now do you believe me?" He felt exhilarated, reckless, terribly happy.

Slowly Darla turned her head and looked straight into his eyes, holding his for a long moment. He felt as if his very soul were drawn and entwined with hers. Stirred beyond anything he had ever known, he found himself moving slowly toward her. He wanted to take her in his arms and hold her fiercely to him, press his lips on hers.

But she must have known what he was about to do, for she suddenly broke the bond between their eyes with a light teasing laugh and turned away.

"All right, Davey boy. You've asked for it. Seven o'clock tomorrow evening, then." She arose from her couch for all the world as if she were a business woman concluding an interview. She couldn't have said any plainer, "Now run along, little boy, I have to dress for my date tonight."

Somehow Dave felt very small and insignificant. But he brushed aside the feeling and departed in a mirage of dazzlement. He had made a date with Darla!

Chapter IX

THE RAIN had stopped and the moon was swaggering high above the city's tallest buildings when Dave came out. It seemed to him that he had been in an enchanted castle. He had no idea how long he had been up there with Darla. He was amazed to hear the clock strike nine. Where had he been planning to go when he met her? Oh, yes, to stay with the little Wrenn boy. Poor kid, he was probably crying with loneliness by now. Dave's heart was warm. He was ready to share his joy with the whole world. He hurried down to Pearl Street.

Davey was overjoyed to see him. The schoolteacher had been there earlier in the evening, straightened things up, and brought him news of his sister. She could come home Thursday evening, but she would not be back at school until next Monday, at the earliest.

"We'll have three whole days together!" the boy exulted. "It's such fun when Anne's home. She can play the best games! Nicer than anybody—except you," he added shyly. "Of course you know more than even Anne—that is, about helicopters and things."

They talked and played awhile but Dave urged the boy to go to sleep soon, for Dave wanted to lie and plan for his date the next evening. He wondered who Darla was going out with tonight. He resented him, whoever he was. Darla had asked *him* to take her out, and that gave him a right in her. His dreams soared.

Out in the country in the dreary old house the two dreary old men were moping, each one muffled closely in his own grievances. But Dave wasn't thinking of them. He was watching himself strut down the corridor of the factory with Darla. The fellows in the drafting room were all turning their heads to look. The foreman himself was bowing and scraping as he introduced Darla. "Yes, yes certainly you may take her through. Show her anything she wants to see." How could even a foreman be hardhearted enough to resist Darla?

The next thing Dave knew, it was broad daylight. Davey Wrenn was watching him eagerly. A big smile broke out on the boy's pale face when he saw that his friend was awake at last.

"Boy! I thought you were going to sleep all day!" cried Davey. "When do you have to go to work?"

"Not until eight o'clock. What time is it? Whew!" he whistled. "It's after seven! Why didn't you wake me? I'll really have to get a move on."

While he hustled through the chores and grabbed a bite of breakfast, Davey was pouring out all the boy-talk that had been piling up while Dave slept. Most of it was about helicopters and jet planes. Dave answered absently. His mind was already straining to get by itself and do its own dreaming about the evening date.

Then Davey reverted to Anne.

"You will bring her home tonight, won't you?" he appealed to Dave.

He spoke with such childish confidence that Dave's heart sank. The boy had no other thought than that Dave was as concerned with Anne and their affairs as he was. Dave hesi-

tated. Any excuse he gave must be a valid one. The thought
of his night school class came into his mind and he started
to say that he never broke in on that for anything. Then he
remembered that he was even at that very moment planning
to skip it for the first time all winter in order to keep his
date with Darla. It had never before seemed a possibility; he
had always been so eager over the work and so anxious to
make good. For the first time he suddenly wondered whether
he had made a terribly wrong move in passing up his class.
He had felt no misgivings about it last night when he was
with Darla, nor even after he left her and fell asleep dreaming of having her for a whole evening to himself. But the
habit he had been forming all winter, of planning all his life
around that class, letting nothing interfere with it, was too
strong for him to break without a qualm. He didn't stop to
think why it was that he preferred not to mention his date
to Davey. A class would seem like a legitimate previous engagement, but to say that he was going out with another
girl, when a person in Anne's condition needed a ride home,
that didn't coincide with Dave's sense of the fitness of things.
The only way out would be if Anne could be brought home
before he went to pick up Darla. He was determined not to
have the date with Darla cut short. He didn't want to set the
appointment with Anne afterwards. That would spoil it all.

Almost impatiently he promised to stop at the hospital
and see about it. Davey was himself so overjoyed that he did
not notice Dave's preoccupation. Dave put Davey's lunch
where he could reach it and went out vaguely depressed over
his dilemma. How was it that he was always getting himself
so involved? He had been a sucker again. Why did he have
any responsibility for this strange girl? She was coming

home; so what? He had a few other things to do besides cart strange girls home from hospitals.

He had barely time to stop and find out what time the patient could be released. They said any time after six o'clock, provided the doctor had been by to okay the dismissal. He usually made his rounds between four and six, so it seemed pretty certain that Dave would be able to pick up Anne and get over to Pearl Street and back in time for his date with Darla.

But how he was to manage that date was the problem. How could he ask for permission to take a guest through the plant, when the office to which he must apply was the same office that kept the records for his night school? The night class was an intensive course, offered by the factory itself. Dave had seized upon it eagerly, knowing that his standing in the class would have a great deal to do with future promotions. The company kept strict tab on absentees. How could a date with a girl possibly be a valid excuse for his failure to appear at class? Why hadn't he realized that when he made the date with Darla? Out of her presence now it seemed a very simple thing to have explained to her about the necessity of perfect attendance at the class. She would have understood. Or would she? He tried to picture himself calling her now to say that he must postpone the date. He could hear her mocking little laugh that stung because it showed she didn't care about him. Well, of course she didn't, not yet. But if he broke his first date, he would certainly not be placing himself in an admirable light.

He put off until the last minute going to the office to apply for permission to take Darla through the plant. He kept hoping that perhaps something would change the picture be-

fore he need ask. When he finally did go, they took his name
and Darla's and told him to wait. After nearly half an hour
he was told that the man in charge had just left and would
be out of town for two or three days. No one else would have
the right to give the permission. He was frantic with chagrin.
Why hadn't he gone earlier? Now he would scarcely have
time to get home and get dressed for the date before he must
be at the hospital for Anne Wrenn. Besides that, his name
was registered as asking for the permission on a school
night, all for nothing. It was bitter. It seemed as if the tangle
was worse instead of better. And where should he take Darla
instead?

He knew he ought to stop at the Park Street Hospital to
see how Aunt Amelia was but that was out of the question
now. He simply had to get home in time to give a press to
his good suit and shine his shoes. Usually he kept his
clothes in immaculate shape but since he had spent so much
time with little Davey, things at home were left undone.

He tore down the busy streets, barely missing a pedestrian
or two. Out on the highway he knew he was going too fast
but it seemed as if he had to keep up with his racing, whirling thoughts. All of a sudden a black car he hadn't noticed
in his mirror appeared beside him and seemed to slow its
pace. Something lurched inside him. His conscience warned
him that it might be a police car. But after a second the black
car picked up more speed and rushed past. Relieved, Dave
eased down to speed limit but his nerves were all the more
on edge. He made the turn into the narrow gateway just too
close and felt his fender grate on the old stone post. Furious
at himself and the world, he jammed his brakes on and got
out to see what damage he had done. There was a long
streak on the right side of the car where the paint was

scraped off entirely. It was just where Darla would notice it as he helped her in. He ground his teeth in rage. *Why* was everything going wrong when he wanted it so much to go right?

Disgusted and discouraged, he roared up the driveway to the porte-cochere and flung himself out. No time tonight even to glance at his pine-covered hill. He so often counted on that long look, to quiet his spirit before the ordeal of facing his father's discontent. But tonight he tore up the stairs three at a time, missing the step once and landing sharply on the one below, thereby shaking his own nerves and his father's, that were already startled by his sudden return.

His father glared as Dave slammed into the bathroom, burst out a moment to set up the ironing board, and then retreated once more to turn on the water full force.

An indignant growl arose in the old man's throat; nobody could hear so it wasn't worth sounding aloud. He bent his eyes to the day-old newspaper he was reading but they saw nothing there, and the paper shook with helpless fury in his hand.

In the twenty minutes or less that it took Dave to bathe and shave, his father conquered the impulse to rant and rage. Cold pride gripped him with frigid silence while Dave got out his good pants and the pressing cloth and carefully deepened the creases. His father stole one gloating look at the boy's straight strong back as he stopped before the blurry mirror at the head of the stairs to make sure his hair was smooth and his tie was lying as it should. Jason was fiercely proud of his boy's good looks, though he would never have let anyone in the world know it.

He was a keen man, for all his grumpiness. He was aware

tonight of the strained expression on Dave's face. Yet he would not ask about it. He would have liked to know about his sister's condition, too, but that would be showing unprecedented interest and his pride again held him from it.

Dave paused an instant before leaping down the stairway. "I'm in a beastly hurry tonight," he explained. "Gotta date and an errand before it. I'll likely be back tonight, though. I won't have to stay in town overnight. Sorry I can't help with supper. I guess there's enough to eat with what I got last night." He was off.

Jason stared after him, bitterly disappointed. It wasn't human to leave a helpless man, half sick, day after day without news of the outside world, not even of his own family! Slowly, viciously, he crushed the old newspaper in his weak fists until tears burned into his eyes and stole down his pale cheeks. A sobbing moan broke the deathly silence and the newspaper fell futilely to the floor. It was a long time before the desolate man made the effort to rise and set about preparing food.

Dave kept stealing a glance at his wrist watch as he raced along. If he could only make it to the hospital by six, and that girl would only be ready on time, he could get her home and be down to Darla's apartment by seven.

He had made up his mind to ask Darla what she would rather do, in view of the fact that the visit to the plant would have to be postponed. He realized that he knew so little of her tastes that he had no idea what entertainment she would prefer, shows, sports, music, or just a ride. He sincerely hoped it might be a ride, not only because he would in a sense have her more to himself and they could get really acquainted, but also because that would be about the cheapest form of entertainment to be had. He had taken the precaution to scrape together every cent he had so as to be prepared for anything within reason, but he was well aware that his idea of a good time and hers might be far apart.

As for dinner, he knew of a nice quiet place overlooking the Potomac, where he had gone once with a wedding party when a friend of his was getting married. He had had little occasion to try out the restaurants, but he knew that most of the good ones were on the river front. It was important to choose one that was fairly reasonable, or he and his father, too, would have to go hungry until next pay day. He was still making payments on his car and there was not much left over for luxuries like eating out.

He had trouble finding a parking place at the hospital so that it was ten minutes after six when he hurried to the desk in the lobby and asked about Anne.

He waited another ten minutes that seemed like ten hours. At last they told him that the doctor had not been by yet to sign Anne's release. He felt his nerves tighten up still more. He had thought that was impossible. Already he felt like a violin tuned too high. He tramped up and down the long reception room. At every turn he consulted his watch. Then he checked it with the clock out in the lobby. Every few minutes he would return to the desk and ask again about Miss Wrenn. Finally, as he turned away for the seventh time, he heard the clerk remark out of the side of her mouth to the telephone operator:

"Sure must be great to have someone that crazy over you. Just wait till they've been married a coupla months, though. It don't last."

That calmed him down somewhat and he was able to grin wryly at himself.

"If they only knew!" he thought to himself. "What if they could see Darla! Brother! They *would* have something to talk about then!"

At last, at twenty minutes of seven when he was all but desperate, deciding that he would have to leave word that he could not possibly wait any longer, Anne stepped out of the elevator.

Dave hardly recognized her at first. She had been so bandaged when he first saw her in the hospital bed and so pale and wan looking the next time that he did not realize that this flowerlike girl who came toward him with such gentle grace was the girl he had first seen in the shabby jalopy. Her soft brown hair hid the wound on her forehead and it was not noticeable that her right shoulder was still tightly bandaged.

She smiled and apologized for keeping him waiting. The doctor had only just been by and signed her permit to go. It was so good of him to offer to take her.

Dave assured her, somewhat reluctantly, that that was quite all right, he was glad to be of help. Inwardly he was seething.

Anne had a midget overnight bag which her teacher friend had brought over with a few of her things. Dave took it and led the way to his car. Anne followed rather slowly. She gave an apologetic laugh as she caught up with him at the car door.

"I guess I'm still a little shaky," she said. "I didn't think that I would be so weak, after such a few days in bed."

Dave realized that he should not have stalked ahead, or else that he should have told her to wait at the hospital door while he brought the car. He was rather ashamed of his thoughtlessness. But he had never learned to admit his failings graciously, so he said nothing. Only the knots inside him grew tighter.

Anne made an attempt to chatter pleasantly on the way to Pearl Street, but as Dave responded very little, and that only glumly, as if occupied with traffic, she finally gave up. She stole a sidelong look at his face: good-looking, yet so hard and tense. She wondered again what had brought that look. It was surely not mere impatience of the moment because she had kept him waiting. It was deep-set, of long standing.

At the house Anne said, "Now you will come up and see Davey, won't you? He sent word he wanted you to stop in. We want to thank you properly for this latest kindness. You don't know how grateful we are."

There was sincerity in her tone, and it suddenly seemed to Dave as if the warmth and cheer that he had found before in that tiny upstairs room had touched him again. It drew him in spite of his haste. For an instant his strain relaxed and almost wistfully he answered, "Oh no, I'm afraid not this time. I have an important—that is—I have—an engagement —an appointment, I mean, and I must hurry. I'll stop some other time to see him. Just tell him hello for me. Thank you just the same. Good night."

He sped away and left Anne standing on the porch looking after him, puzzled.

Several times during his pacing of the hospital reception room, Dave had gone to the public phone and tried to get Darla to tell her that he might be a few minutes late. But every time he had called, her line was busy. Now he took another look at his watch. Almost half-past seven!

It would be ten minutes before he could reach her apartment house. Better call her and explain. If she was angry it would give her time to cool off. She would know that he had tried, anyway. Surely she would understand that one cannot hurry doctors and hospitals. After all, it was for her sake that he had contacted Anne Wrenn in the first place.

He parked outside a drugstore and ran in, dialing frantically. He could hear her phone ring and ring, but there was no answer!

Dave felt as if all the pegs of the violin strings had slipped at once and left him loose and dangling. He scarcely knew what to do or where to go. But his mind had been set for so many tense hours on that apartment building that it seemed as if he must push on and get there no matter what the discouragements. So he started his car once more and made his way to the park.

The liveried flunkey at Chez Villon informed him that Miss Dartman had left word just a few minutes ago that if a young man called he should be told that she would return shortly. Would he please wait?

"Shortly." What did that mean? Dave settled himself in a modernistic lobby chair and tried to make some sort of sense out of the day.

Nothing had gone right all day long. For one thing, he had been reprimanded at work, the first time that had ever happened. It rankled. He had made mistakes that he should not have made. He could not seem to think clearly. That was when he began to tighten up. Or had he begun before that, and the mistakes occurred because he was already tense? He didn't know. All that was plain to him now was that he had missed the boat on everything all day. And now came the thought with a deep stab that he was missing his class, and for nothing. He had thought it worth while to miss it for an evening with Darla. But he was not even getting that. He wanted to blame everything on that sick girl who had had to be brought home. He found himself thinking bitter thoughts about her, calling her selfish and presumptuous. He knew that wasn't true, though. Where was the trouble, then? There must be something radically wrong somewhere. Things couldn't get into such a mess all by themselves, when you were trying your best to do the decent, right, kind thing. It was just as Dad always said. Everything was unfair.

He should go to see Aunt Amelia too. She might be conscious now. Well, surely Uncle Harry would have been in to see her by this time. She was his wife. Let him look after her.

Then came the thought of the little boy who, Dave knew, had been looking forward to his coming home with his sister. He would have liked to see that greeting when the sister walked in. He knew he had disappointed Davey and he felt inwardly ashamed.

Dave looked at his watch. After eight. His class had already started. Hadn't he better go now, before it was too late? But what if Darla should come and find that he had not waited as she left word for him to do? She would accuse him of not coming at all, maybe. He must let her see that he cared to please her. He got up and walked restlessly back and forth, up and down the gardened walk outside the building.

Nine o'clock. Class was over. He went to the lobby again and sat down.

The elevator noiselessly opened its impassive mouth. Out stepped Darla, gay and smiling in black satin and diamonds, chattering lightheartedly to a tall middle-aged man in the uniform of a colonel. Dave's heart turned over and squeezed hard. His head seemed several feet above his body. He couldn't get himself together. Darla saw him and came toward him laughing, that mocking laugh. She introduced her friend as "Colonel Exmore." Dave bowed solemnly and turned to Darla to apologize for being late. But Darla paid no attention to him, merely shrugged and said carelessly, "Too bad, dear boy. Another time. Good night, now," and sauntered out with the colonel.

All the disappointments of all day seemed to flow back upon Dave in a rush that made him stagger. It took self-control to walk quietly out of the building and over to his car. He could see taillights disappearing down the drive. The driver wore a visored cap and a lovely lady's head was outlined quite close beside him.

Dave watched it out of sight.

His class was over now. He had missed it. For what?

Chapter X

Anne had to rest awhile on each step as she climbed the steep flight up to the back bedroom. Her weakness shocked her. She found even the tiny overnight bag a drag on her. She wished that nice-looking young man had stayed at least long enough to carry it up for her. But he had other things to do, of course. He had been most kind to take the time to bring her home.

One step after another she struggled up. Near the top she heard Davey's eager voice.

"Anne? Oh, Anne, is that you?"

She must not let the boy know how weak she was. She put forth all her effort and made the last two steps, gasping for breath at the top.

She managed a short cheery sound like an answer to Davey's call and then took another slow, deep breath. Setting her lips firmly and forcing herself to breathe slowly, she put on a smile and entered the room.

Davey's face was alight and his arms were outstretched.

She sank on his bed and he hugged her tightly, planting a clumsy kiss on her left ear.

"Careful Davey," she warned, "I'm not quite whole yet." But they laughed together for joy.

With a catch in his voice Davey said:

"Wasn't God good to let you come home so soon, and to send that nice big Dave to take care of me. Boy, we had lots of fun. Where is he?"

"He had to go, Davey. Yes, he was most kind. I don't even know him. Who is he? Did he tell you anything about himself?"

"Oh yes, I know all about him," replied Davey confidently. "He works in the helicopter factory at the Naval Research place. You remember it. The week before I got sick we passed it once and I asked you what it was." Anne nodded. "But I don't think he knows the Lord," added Davey with a troubled look.

"What makes you think so?" questioned Anne.

"Well, I talked a little about Him and he didn't seem interested. I think anybody who knew Him would sort of show it somehow, don't you? And he said he didn't ever pray about things."

"How did he come to tell you that?" asked Anne.

"I asked him," answered Davey simply.

"Well, suppose we pray for him, then," suggested Anne.

"Ho!" cried Davey. "Of course. I have been, ever since. I think that's why God sent him here. Maybe nobody else was doing any praying for him and it's a way we can thank him for helping us." Davey went on to chatter about his airplanes and tell all he had learned about the helicopters. He showed his sister the new little model that Dave had brought him and Anne silently thanked the Lord for sending such a decent, kindly young man who so perfectly fitted their need at the time. She kept seeing, however, the hard, bitter look Dave's face had worn every time she had seen him. What could have caused it? Only the Lord could deal with a condition like that.

Wearily she managed to get together enough for them both to eat, gave a feeble massage to Davey's legs and then dropped exhausted into bed, thankful to be home again.

Dave drove blindly, carelessly, through the park and across the city, past the Naval Air Station and Bolling Field, on out to the country road that led up the hill to the big house that was supposed to be home.

With bitter distaste he turned in once more at the stone posts, remembering with a pang the paint that was no more on the side of his precious car. What a day! Was there anything that could go wrong that had gone right?

He climbed out and closed the car door. Feeling desperately the need of something or someone beyond himself, out of habit he looked off toward the hill of pines. It was black there now, with sharp spikes of firs like saw teeth edging the skyline. But as he watched, suddenly a rim of gold appeared. It seemed to turn the trees to feathery velvet and in only a matter of moments the whole dark mysterious scene softened and shone bright under the limpid, liquid moonlight. The village at the foot of the hill lay in quiet order. Even the Home for the Aged and Infirm across the valley by the river shone like a silver palace. Something like hope stole into Dave's heart. Maybe things were dark or bright all according to the way you saw them. But the way ahead for him surely did look dark. Was there a light anywhere that could flood the path for him and show him the way out of his maze?

Dave was about to go into the house when he heard voices. That was unprecedented. Nobody ever talked around the place. That was one of the things Dave hated about it, the deathlike silence. His father never had anything much to say except a grumble occasionally, or a long mumbling dissertation to his son about politics. That was in the evenings when Dave was trying to study. Aunt Amelia and Uncle Harry never held what might be called conversation.

A question about the hens, or an impatient reminder to bring in the milk or put some tools away, that was all Dave ever heard them say to each other. He often wondered why people wanted to live together when they seemed to have so little in common. Many a time in his youth he had tried to imagine his aunt and uncle when they were young and falling in love with one another. He had given up trying.

It was unusual for neighbors or even salesmen to bother to climb the last steep part of the hill to have any social contact with the three oldsters there. A few had tried: the Dawsons, when they first moved into the next farmhouse, down the hill and across the road; the Fennings before them. But people rarely came twice; they were soon bored by the family grievance recitals. Even Aunt Amelia's minister never pretended to make a pastoral call.

Dave paused at the doorway. Those were men's voices. One was his father's. It had the angry, resentful tone that he always used. Was the other Uncle Harry? That was hard to believe. Dad and Uncle Harry hadn't spoken for years.

Dave stood with his head cocked, listening. He preferred not to get into a family row tonight. He would rather take a walk in the moonlight until it was over. As he stood so, his eyes caught the gleam of chrome on a car parked outside the stone gateposts, across the rise of the hill. He hadn't noticed it when he came in, he was so preoccupied. Its outlines showed it to be a late model of a fine car. Someone had chosen to make it on foot the rest of the way up to the house rather than attempt the narrow gateway.

Dave squinted, trying to find something familiar about the automobile. Perhaps it might be one of Aunt Amelia's acquaintances.

Softly Dave turned the doorknob. He planned to slide up the stairs quietly. Perhaps his father would not hear him.

He slipped inside and put one foot on the lowest stair, balancing by the carved mahogany newel post. But the door to the seldom-used living room was open and a light clearly reflected the visitor in a long gilt-framed pier glass in the hall.

Seated in a straight antique chair was a middle-aged gentleman with smooth-fitting white hair and a smooth-fitting black suit. The collar showed a wide, gleaming white band in front. It must be Aunt Amelia's pastor! He must have heard of the accident. Well, it was decent of him to show some interest in her at last.

Dave hesitated on the bottom step. He had no desire to talk to the man, but he was mildly curious to see what sort of person he was who had stayed so consistently away from his parishioner until now. The visitor was an oval-shaped man of about fifty. His clean pink face seemed to bulge slightly in the middle, and his form did the same. Even his pink-rimmed pale blue eyes had a sort of bulgy look. He wore a wide smile full of large plump teeth. Dave wondered what he was talking about. Surely something very pleasant, for he maintained his pleased composure even in the face of Jason Truscott's grumpy rejoinders.

"It might work out very conveniently for all concerned, you know, Mr. Truscott," he beamed. "As you must be well aware, this property is no longer desirable to the average buyer. It would take a vast amount to put it into livable shape. . . ."

"We manage to live here all right," sputtered Jason.

"Ah yes, of course. Yes, I meant no offense. But after all,

it is your own old homestead, as it were, and one puts up with things in a case like that. But when it comes to a—ah —gracious living, shall we say?—it would cost a great deal to modernize it sufficiently. Besides, most people today, even the wealthy, are not seeking such a large place as this. If they want it, they build it new for themselves. Now our suggestion is this, that since our denomination has allotted this certain sum of money toward a home for the indigent of our church, why not let us lease the place for, say seventy-five dollars a month. That, I am told is the very top sum you could hope to get. We would do what little would need to be done for poor people to live in it in a fair degree of comfort, and we would allow you and your sister to remain here as long as you live. That would supply you with a certain dwelling for life, without cost, as we would be willing to pay all utilities, and upon the death of you and your sister the place would go to the church, thereby," the visitor clasped his hands together in satisfaction, "assuring you a star in your crown for your splendid contribution to the church." The wide smile grew wider as the idea grew upon the man. He caressed his hands again as if congratulating himself.

Jason did not answer. His shiny eyes were black points, leveled directly at the other man.

"You see," continued the clergyman, "it was only when I heard of your sister's unfortunate accident that it suddenly occurred to me that here might be the solution to our problem. Our committee has been searching for some time, quite fruitlessly, for a suitable property. I'm sure you can realize how splendid the plan would be for all concerned, insuring you as it does, a monthly stipend, to be divided between you and your sister according to any agreement you and she

would care to make, of course. What more would you want?
As the Apostle said, 'having food and raiment, let us there-
with be content.'" He laughed as if he had said something
rather cute.

"*Rich* food, *fine* raiment, *and* a handsome car in your
own case," Dave felt like adding. But he kept his mouth
shut and remained in the shadows of the hall. Somehow,
much as he had always hated the old tumbledown house,
he suddenly found himself resenting this sleek well-heeled
stranger who was presuming to take it and plan their lives
for them. He had often wished his father had a small in-
come or pension for then there would not be the strain
upon himself to provide for him, but this scheme sounded
to him like something akin to robbery. Polite, charitable
robbery, yet definitely a plan which would benefit this man's
church, and by which it could acquire a twelve-acre property for practically nothing. If his father fell for it, Dave
would be greatly surprised, if only for the reason that his
father opposed anything nowadays that anybody at all suggested.

But even Dave was not prepared for his father's reaction.

With great difficulty Jason got to his feet. He had been a
tall man before his illness, and now he seemed to straighten
up, towering above the plump smile that still beamed up at
him with placid assurance.

Jason had not taken a step without his cane since his last
attack, but now he planted his trembling feet firmly, and
slowly raised his cane, pointing toward the door. His face
was livid with fury.

"You—you damned *rascal!*" he roared hoarsely. "GET
OUT!" Then all at once Jason crumpled and subsided in a
pitiful heap on the hardwood parquetry floor.

With a cry of alarm Dave rushed in and knelt over him, paying not the slightest heed to the visitor. He listened to his heart and detecting a weak beat he lifted his father gently to the old-fashioned couch and tore upstairs for medicine. He soon came flying down again and gave his father a few drops, but there was no response.

Frantically he rushed out of the house, calling back to the minister, "I'm going across to the Dawsons' to phone for the doctor. You stay there with him." It did not occur to him that he had given peremptory orders to the pastor of the largest, most wealthy church in all that section. In fact he never gave the man a thought.

In a very few minutes he came tearing back. The sleek visitor stood wringing his hands, his back to the man who had so unceremoniously requested him to leave.

"Is he—ah—that is, he's still living, is he?" he asked nervously.

"Yes," answered Dave curtly, after a breathless look, "but he is very sick."

"Ah, poor man. Well, I was just going to say, my boy, that if he *should* go, you know—of course nobody exactly anticipates such an eventuality, but if you should suddenly find yourself the—ah—heir of this property, if you know what I mean, why, you will know where to go for a very good proposition on it. We will be glad to make you the same offer, if you know what I mean."

"I certainly do know too well what you mean," blazed Dave, "and my opinion entirely coincides with my father's. Good night." He turned on his heel leaving his visitor to make his own way out.

As the hours dragged by and the doctor did not arrive, Dave thought once of going for Uncle Harry. But what

```
EOE                    FC        $

JEWELLED SWORD
HILL R            HRV 0890815658
PAPER       ABK


       089-081-5658      QTY_____


ARK BOOK AND GIFT OF SEYMOUR
0001047                    730487-1

           6-23-87
```

good would that do? If he asked him to go to Dawsons' and call another doctor he might refuse. No, he decided he would rather be alone.

His father was motionless. It was most obviously another stroke.

Dave had never felt so alone in all his life. Even poor old Aunt Amelia wasn't around to talk to.

It was half-past eleven when he was suddenly startled by a sound unusual for that place.

Chapter XI

Like bird songs bubbling up, lighthearted, carefree, came the sound of whistling, up the drive and onto the porch. Whoever it was walked with firm, confident step, unhurried, and yet eager.

Dave was alert at once. He hastened to the door.

There stood a stranger, middle-aged, a little over average height, solid as a football player. His hair, slightly gray and thinning on top, was awry as if it had been some time since he had had opportunity to pay any attention to it, but his clothes were well tailored, clean, and freshly pressed. In his hand he carried a doctor's kit and that made Dave draw a breath of relief.

The thing about the man which impressed Dave most was his smile, so different from the bland empty smile of the clerical visitor who had been there earlier in the evening. He seemed to light up the dim dreary hallway and reach in and warm Dave through and through.

"Barnhart's my name," said the stranger. "I've taken over Dr. Porter's practice. You sent for me?" Dave nodded and led the doctor to the couch in the living room where he had tried to make his father as comfortable as possible.

With big hands that were gentle as a mother's the doctor examined Mr. Truscott, while Dave sketched briefly the history of his illnesses.

It was not long before he leaned back and looked up at

Dave still standing tensely at the foot of the couch. His smile was not brilliant now, but rather tender and full of sympathy.

"You know that it's another stroke?" he said.

Dave nodded again.

"It's his fourth, you say? He may come out of it and he may not." He spoke slowly, gently. "His age counts for him. He is a young man yet. Who will be caring for him? Is there someone here all the time?"

Dave thought of Uncle Harry but shook his head, no.

"It's not that there's much nursing to be done for him," explained the doctor, "but he should have care and constant watching for a while."

"I can't hire a nurse, but I have carried hospitalization for him since his last illness," said Dave.

"That would be the thing for him, then, at least for two or three weeks. He may be well enough by then to be brought home, if you can arrange to have someone around here. A practical nurse would do."

Dave seemed to wilt. "How much do they charge?" he asked. "I've heard that even practical nurses are pretty steep. I don't know how I'd manage."

"They aren't cheap," smiled the doctor. "Well, we'll see how things are after a few weeks. Maybe something can be worked out. I'll pray about it." He smiled again, that heart-warming smile. Dave thought surely if anybody's prayers would be heard it would be those of a man like this who was willing to come out late at night. Many doctors nowadays would have refused.

"You seem different," he said impulsively. "More like the old-fashioned doctors people used to write about in books."

Dr. Barnhart laughed. "I'm just a good-for-nothing, no-account old sinner like anybody," he said, "but I have a great God. I tell you, young fellow—what's your name?"

"Dave Truscott."

"Dave, when you know the Lord Jesus Christ as your Saviour, and let Him run your life, you are bound to be different. Do you know Him?"

Dave hesitated, stammered, and said, "I haven't gone to church for ten years, sir, ever since my mother died."

"I'm not talking about going to church, Dave. Lots of people go to church who don't know the Lord. Even some ministers don't know Him."

"You can say *that* again," Dave burst out. "There was a chiseling old scoundrel in here tonight trying to pull a fast deal on us. That's what gave Dad his stroke, he got so mad at him."

Dr. Barnhart shook his head. "There are plenty like that, but not all. When you get your eyes on them you get to doubting God and everything that's good. We have to keep our eyes on the Lord Jesus Christ. You will never find anything in Him that will disappoint you."

"Ye-es?" responded Dave questioningly. "I'm afraid you are talking to the wrong person. I've always tried to live right and all that, but I don't go in for religion. I've seen too many hypocrites."

"Dave, I'm not talking about religion either. There are a lot of 'religions'! They all tell you to *do* something or other to get to heaven. But God so loved the world that, knowing man couldn't do anything to help himself, *God* did it *all*. He sent His Son, the Lord Jesus Christ, into this world to take all the guilt of all of us. He died *for* us, Dave, and He said that whoever believes that, is righteous in His sight and *has* eternal life. Oh, He's a great Saviour. You need Him,

Dave. I can see you have a pretty rugged road to travel. You're discouraged, aren't you?"

Dave choked back tears that suddenly started at the man's sympathy. He hadn't had anyone care whether things were hard or not for so long that he had forgotten how good it felt. It must be the hard day that made him so childish. He gave a shamed laugh and tried to say, "It's been a tough day," but the words ended in something like a sob and he felt more ashamed of himself than ever.

But Dr. Barnhart didn't laugh. He laid a brotherly hand on his shoulder. "I know, Dave. I wonder if it's ever occurred to you to thank the Lord for getting you down like this where you are completely discouraged? I know you are. I could see it when I came in. And it's not just your father's illness, either, is it?"

Dave shook his head. The man's kindness had unnerved him. He couldn't get his voice.

"I had somewhat the same experience some years ago," went on the doctor. "I had been a good fellow, too. Oh, I took a drink now and then, but I never got drunk. I was brought up in a good Christian home. I even went to church and taught a Sunday School class for a while. I thought I was pretty good. And then things began to happen. I lost my job. I thought I was going to lose my wife and family. And a lot of other things got me down so that I didn't care whether I lived or not. Then one day some really terrible things happened and I was at the end of my rope. I had *nobody* but the Lord to go to. And that was the place He had been getting me to all the time. As soon as I gave up and admitted where I had been wrong and let Him run my life, He began to solve all the problems. That's grace! Undeserved kindness! Dave, with Christ you *can't lose!* 'He that hath the Son hath life, but he that hath not the Son of God hath not life.' Without Him you can't win.

"I must go now for there's another emergency waiting for me, but here," he reached in his inner pocket and took out a folded slip of paper, "read this, and if you have a Bible, read the Gospel of John. You'll find Jesus Christ there. Good night now, and God bless you, Dave. He has His hand on you, I'm sure. He doesn't let trouble come just for fun. There's a purpose in all this. I'll arrange for the hospital room right away and send you word through the Dawsons. Good-bye, Dave." He took Dave's hand in a firm, warm grasp and strode off the porch to his car, whistling again.

Dave watched him go down the drive and for the first time in his life he felt as if he had a real friend.

He went over and stood looking down at his father, frozen in that rigid, deathlike silence. What had his father ever got out of life by his critical, resentful attitude? What if his father had been like this doctor? Dave could not imagine what it would be to have been the child of such a father as Dr. Barnhart.

All at once, as Dave gazed at his father's face, the eyes opened and looked at him. They were tortured eyes, but there was intelligence in them. The lids soon dropped shut and did not open again but Dave wondered whether his father had heard all that had been said.

Dave was still holding in his hand the little leaflet that he had accepted absent-mindedly from the doctor. He looked down at the printed page now.

"Why are You in the Dark?" was its title.

Yes, why? wondered Dave. Could it be that there was any truth in what Dr. Barnhart said? Or was he just another kindhearted quack? He would like to watch the man for a time and see whether he was real, or whether the shine would rub off. As soon as he had time Dave planned to read the little tract, but now he must gather a few things together for his father. They would be sending for him soon. How strange that after so many years the ambulance was making two trips in one week to the old house! Aunt Amelia might be surprised to wake up tomorrow and find her despised brother in the next room.

So he tucked the leaflet in his pocket and ran upstairs. Nothing in his circumstances was changed, yet it seemed as if bright hope were stealing into his life. It reminded him of that moonlight that had so quietly and unexpectedly taken possession of the dark landscape outside. How strange that the words of that title should be about the darkness, implying that there was light somewhere. Well, if there was, he surely hoped he would find it soon.

He packed a small box with necessities for his father and then carried a mattress down to the living room. He would have to go to work tomorrow and he must snatch a little sleep if he could before time to go to the hospital. It might be a couple of hours or more before they would send the ambulance.

Miles away across the city Anne Wrenn was lying awake. The pain in her shoulder had come on again after trying to give Davey his massage and she could not sleep. It seemed as if one problem after another kept pouncing upon her weary mind. Her school job. How was she ever to get strength to go back and finish the year? And would she do well enough so that she would get a regular teaching position next year? The State Board was tightening its regulations and it was possible that she might be required to go to summer school in order to make good her certification. How could she possibly do that? She couldn't. She had stretched every penny so as to save enough to live on during the summer. Now that little bit would soon be gone. What sort of job could she get that would keep her and Davey the three months till school began, *if* she did get a school teaching job? Round and round she went on that theme until she finally remembered that God had the solution and in despair she committed it to Him, assured that as He had already provided He would continue to do so.

But no sooner had she laid down her cares about money than she began to be troubled about Davey's health. Was she right in remaining with the doctor who was tending Davey at present? He had been recommended by several people as the best in the city. He was rather expensive, but could she trust anyone else when it might mean all the difference for Davey between lying a helpless cripple and living a normal life? That one was too much, too, and she finally rolled it onto the Lord as she knew she ought to have done in the beginning.

Then a wave of thankfulness swept over her for the unknown young man who had so kindly stayed with Davey the two nights she was away. Who but God could have found, out of the hundreds of thousands in that big city, a man who would be willing and able and so perfectly fitted not only to care for but also to entertain her little air-minded brother? Who was the young man? Davey hadn't discovered much about him. It was enough for the child that his new nurse knew something about planes and helicopters, and had brought him a model to make. He must be a good man!

But Anne wondered about him. Not that she questioned his integrity, but he had admitted to Davey that he was not a Christian, and it was not usual for even a Christian who was a perfect stranger to show such kindness. The only reason that common sense could offer was that he had been sent by the driver of that other car to smooth the troubled waters and obviate a heavy lawsuit. That made her indignant. But in spite of herself Anne could not forget the tense, strained sadness of the young man's face. So at last, as she had done with the other two problems, she presented the whole matter to the Lord and prayed earnestly for the kind young man whom God had sent to help them in their time of need.

At that moment the kind young man was racing into town again, following his father in the ambulance. He was feeling anything but kind, and not even young. He felt as if all the weight of everybody's troubles had descended to him.

Just now he was puzzling over what in the world he would do when both the cantankerous invalids returned home. He couldn't possibly hire nurses for them both. Aunt Amelia would unquestionably have to have one. Even if Uncle Harry could or would nurse her, Dave doubted if she would put up with him. Suppose she did relax the purse strings enough to hire a nurse, would she be willing to let the woman look after his father part time? That he also doubted. Even if she didn't really need her every minute, Aunt Amelia was mean enough to contrive extra things to keep her busy so as to get her money's worth out of her. Dave had no fond delusions about his family. He pitied the poor unfortunate nurse who should have the task of caring for two such fretful, demanding patients, though his father would not be able to fret, of course, until he was able to talk. How strange and how fitting that such a malady had attacked him, Dave thought. If he did believe in a God, how suitable for God to choose such a way of punishment for a man who had used his power of speech for nothing but railing. But would it do any good? Dad had been taken this way before and he was even worse afterwards. If God did have anything to do with it, it didn't look as if He were accomplishing very much.

Dave thought again of the radiant man who had come at his call so late at night. It was as if he had lit up the whole place with his joyous smile. Why weren't there more people like him?

The thought of Darla finally pushed itself into his notice. He had tried to avoid the memory of the evening's disappointment for it was too much for him to understand and he felt he had enough to struggle with already. She doubtless had no idea of how she had hurt him with her indifference. Probably the colonel was some important person who had turned up unexpectedly. That must have been it. And she couldn't very well explain right in front of him.

By the time Dave reached the hospital he had freely forgiven Darla for her apparent rudeness to him and the sting of the broken date was eased somewhat.

After making arrangements for his father, Dave stopped at the desk to see how Aunt Amelia was. It was nearly six o'clock in the morning and the night clerk was just going off duty. She looked up the name, glanced at a slip of paper and said, "As well as could be expected," which of course told him nothing except that she was still alive. He would have to stop after work that afternoon to see his father, so he would look in on Aunt Amelia then. He was beginning to feel quite at home in the hospital.

He had nothing to do now until eight, except to get some

breakfast, so he decided to take a long way home and drive past the apartment in Rock Creek Park. It gave him a thrill just to look up at "her" window and know that she was there. And now that there was nothing unpleasant between them, at least on his part, he could dream as he rode by of some future time when he might be allowed to see her there, or perhaps take her out to dinner. It had happened once, it could happen again. He had rationalized away any fault in her. She was perfect as far as he was concerned.

The birds and the milkmen were just beginning the business of the day when Dave approached the huge apartment house where Darla lived.

A car ahead of him rolled along rather erratically and Dave slowed down. The driver might be drunk. Then the car ahead came to a halt at the entrance to the apartment house and the light was clear enough to see that the driver wore a United States uniform. Dave caught his breath in anger and horror. Was that Darla who was getting out of the car? And the colonel most obviously *was* drunk! Darla hastened into the building and the colonel started on, as uncertainly as before. There were two others in the back seat, a tall, angular-looking girl and another man in a dress suit.

Who was this colonel, anyway, who dared to take out a girl like Darla when he wasn't fit to drive? And how dared he keep her out all night? Dave was determined to discover something about him. He followed the car as it wove crazily back and forth around the curves of the park. At times it would proceed fairly well but then at the worst turns it would careen toward a culvert, or run up over a curbing.

The car finally stopped at a handsome house on swank Sixteenth Street to let out the other girl. The men drove on and Dave still followed until they reached a more modest section of the city, where they drew up, handed the car over to a uniformed attendant, and went into a hotel.

What good he had done in following, Dave didn't know, only he had satisfied something in himself that rose up in indignation at that man.

Dave was completely oblivious of a plain black car that had trailed him through all the devious ways and still kept at a distance behind when he started at last for home.

Chapter XII

Weary as he was, Dave drove to the hospital that afternoon when his work was over. He found his father's condition unchanged, so he looked in on Aunt Amelia. She was keeping two or three nurses and an interne in a dither trying to get her comfortable.

"She'll get well all right," he muttered to himself. "She's back on her high horse again."

The traction on her leg was not right, she complained, and she was positive that it was forcing the bones out of position. She was so taken up with the inefficiency and carelessness of the hospital attendants that she scarcely noticed Dave. She accepted his coming as a matter of course and tried to put him to work, too, running hither and yon, calling for this nurse and that doctor. But Dave knew his aunt of old and during the first errand she sent him on, he quietly stepped into the elevator and disappeared. She was antagonizing every attendant on the floor. Soon she would have everyone avoiding her calls. But you couldn't stop her. How well he knew!

For the first time in years Dave was free from the feeling that he must get home and see to his father. Not that he was glad his father was sick, but it had been a heavy bondage. He thought of trying to see Darla but decided that he was still too angry and disgusted with that colonel friend of hers to go back yet.

At the plant that day they had given out some little anniversary souvenirs in the form of helicopter models. Most of the fellows had grabbed for them to take home to their children. Dave had thought of Davey, with a little thrill to think of the pleasure the boy would take in it. So instead of going back to the dreary house with nobody in it but Uncle Harry, he drove eagerly to Pearl Street.

But he was not prepared for the ecstatic delight of little Davey when Anne opened the door and the boy saw who it was.

"It's Big Dave!" He whooped with glee and seized on the model, examining it and asking innumerable questions. He talked so fast that Anne had no opportunity to put in a word.

Once Dave looked up and caught her glance upon him, puzzled, wondering. Perhaps she thought it strange of him to come. Well, he certainly wasn't chasing after *her*. She needn't think he was. Oh, she was attractive enough, with her soft blondy-brown hair, her big brown eyes and her dainty ways. But this visit was strictly for the boy's pleasure. His conversation was addressed almost exclusively to him.

"It's getting to be wonderful weather these days, Davey. Didn't you tell me once that the doctor said you might take a ride sometime?"

Davey's eyes grew big like his sister's and Anne's face glowed.

"Oh, Big Dave!" cried the boy. "That would be wonderful. You could carry me down, couldn't you?"

"Yes, if your sister agrees," said Dave. He was a little hesitant before this girl. She was not one with whom a stranger might take liberties. She had turned down the man who roomed down the hall. She might do the same with him.

But Anne was overjoyed. It made Dave feel just a little

encouraged. It was almost like having a family who trusted you.

"Suppose we make it tomorrow afternoon, then, shall we? I have Saturday afternoons off. Is that convenient to you both?"

They assured him that it was, and then Davey spoke up.

"Anne, can't Big Dave stay and have supper with us? He'd even get it for you, wouldn't you?" he confidently appealed to Dave as if he were the child's personal property. "You know he has got meals here before. He's not just a regular stranger."

Anne smiled. "We would be very glad to have him stay, Davey, but you know I don't have anything here for a company supper."

"Oh, please, don't make company of me," laughed Dave. "I won't stay if you do."

"All right, then," urged Davey. "He'll stay. He practically said he would."

They all laughed and Dave sat down again on the edge of Davey's bed and began to show him some tricks.

Anne set up a card table, almost on top of him, to be sure, but Dave didn't mind, and in a few minutes she had a delectable-looking supper of creamed chicken on toast, fresh-frozen peas, and tall glasses of iced tea for the grownups, with milk instead for Davey.

As they gathered round to enjoy it, Davey looked up at Anne. "May I say thank you for it, tonight?"

Anne smiled. "Yes, if you like, Davey."

He bowed his head and very simply gave thanks for the food and for "Big Dave."

Then he opened his eyes and said to Dave:

"You see, I wanted to be sure to thank the Lord for sending you back here. I was afraid Anne wouldn't do it."

Anne blushed and said, "Oh Davey!" and Dave tried to pretend he didn't hear but a twinkle was in his eyes. He turned the subject quickly to airplanes again and Davey was off on a siege of questions once more.

Dave thought to himself that it was one of the oddest situations he had ever been in, but one of the most enjoyable. He tried to analyze it on the way home. It wasn't the food, certainly, though that had tasted very good after years of canned fare of his own concocting. It wasn't merely the presence of Anne, though she did seem nice and it was pleasant to have a woman around. But somehow it reminded him of one summer day in the distant past that he had always treasured in his memory. Both his parents had taken him to visit relatives, a rare event. While the older folk were talking, his young cousin, a boy about his own age, had taken him on a stroll through the woods to the boy's favorite spot, a quiet pool encircled by fir trees. The place was shielded from the hot sun; only a sifting of light touched the pool and made it seem to laugh with silent delight. A bird sang in full view where they could watch his joy. The boys slipped out of their clothes and slid into the cool water. A long time they dived and floated, the green lace of the branches gently waving like a canopy above them. Then they climbed to a rock where they could look down into a bluebird's nest. Two baby birds were there asleep, snuggled close to each other, and their mother. Dave still remembered how he had envied the little featherlings, secure beneath the mother's wings.

That day his father and mother had seemed at peace with each other. It was a day that proved to his childish mind that such things could be. He used to use it as a dream to go to sleep on at night, lonely times when his mother had left them and his father was cross and sullen.

His sunset display was on when he reached home, and he drank it in, thinking of the gorgeous beauty of Darla Ray Dartman. Would he ever see her again? He sighed as the colors faded. Then he went upstairs to try to bring some cleanliness and order out of the careless mess his father had left.

After scrubbing and scouring as well as he could, Dave sat down to read the paper. But there was nothing that particularly interested him. He read the results of various games over the country, glanced at the world news headlines, passed over a few murder trials, and threw the paper down.

What a dull, dreary place! Then he suddenly remembered the little leaflet that Dr. Barnhart had given him. He reached in his pocket and drew it out.

"Why are You in the Dark?"

There was a picture on the front under the title. It showed a man feeling his way along a narrow dark path that had a steep precipice at one side and boulders ahead.

Dave turned it over, actually to see how long the article was. On the back page there was no reading, only another picture. The same man was walking confidently along the same path, but now he held a flashlight in his hand and the way was plain between the boulders.

"Hunh!" grunted Dave. "Looks like an ad for Ever Bright Batteries or something."

He turned again to the inside page. It began like a story.

Once upon a time there was a certain man who started out to go to a distant city. He was not sure of the way, and nobody seemed to have a map. He asked many people for directions but they all told him different paths. He tried several but every one led to a dead end.

He inquired and discovered that he was not the only one who wished to travel to that city. Many intended going. But still he found no one who knew the way.

It grew darker and darker. He seemed to make no progress. He asked again of his fellow travelers. Many said, "Yes, it will be dark all the way. You can't expect to know the path. Just do the best you can."

But after struggling along desperately for some time he thought he saw a dim ray of light. He hastened toward it and found that it belonged to a man standing beside the road. He had a large supply of lights and maps. He offered them to everyone who would take them.

"They are very costly," he told them, "but I am offering them free to all who are traveling to the city."

Still the majority of travelers simply looked at him strangely and groped on.

When the poor wanderer found he could obtain light and a map, he took them gladly and went on his way with confidence, rejoicing.

That was all, except two lines in bold type at the bottom of the page: "Jesus said, I am the Way, the Truth and the Life. No man cometh unto the Father but by Me." "In Him is life; and the life is the light of men."

Dave read it through and then read it again. Then he turned to the cover page once more: "Why are You in the Dark?"

"Well, why am I? Are we all fools?"

He sat a long time thinking. The simple little tale seemed very real to him. It even seemed as if he could recognize the features of the man at the side of the road—he looked just like that doctor who had come last night through the darkness to help him. What made that man so different?

"He that hath the Son hath life, but he that hath not the Son of God hath not life." Dave read the words over and shuddered. Could that be the matter with most of the people he knew? Was that the matter with *him?* He was seized with a nameless fear and he actually trembled. He surely didn't want to lose out on this great thing, whatever it was that the doctor and little Davey had. He forgot all about his arguments. He suddenly saw himself as one of those aimless foolish travelers, groping in the dark. With a cry of terror he arose and dropped to his knees beside the chair. He had never prayed before in his life. He didn't know how. But the words tore out of his heart.

"Oh God! I don't understand any of this, but I know I'm in the dark. Help me. Give me light and show me the way."

His shoulders heaved with the sudden realization of his great need.

That was all. He stayed on his knees several minutes. He had not expected to see a great light, nor hear voices. He did not have any particular feeling when he finally arose, only there was a calm in his heart. The terror was gone. He seemed to see again that quiet pool and hear the bird songs.

Wait. *Was* he a little balmy? He thought he had imagined the bird songs. But he certainly heard something, a real sound like bird songs. It was the doctor's whistle!

With a heart strangely light he ran downstairs.

He didn't know that the change in his own face was almost as startling as the radiance he had noticed in the doctor's the night before.

Dr. Barnhart grasped his hand warmly. Dave beamed, and the doctor looked at him keenly.

"You don't seem like the same boy I met here last night," he said.

Dave gave another radiant smile. "I—I guess I'm not!" he said. "I just—"

"Go on," encouraged the doctor, "you just what?"

Dave gave an embarrassed little laugh.

"I don't know how to say it! I just asked the Lord to—to give me light, and I guess He has!"

"Of course He has," grinned the doctor. "He always does what He says He will. Now do you know *who* the light is, Dave?"

"I don't know what you mean, sir."

"Do you have a Bible, Dave?"

"No, sir, I'm ashamed to say I don't. That is, there may be one in the house somewhere but I've never come on it."

"Come here and sit down and let's look at what God says," said the older man, drawing a small much-used Bible from his coat pocket.

He turned to the Gospel of John and pointed to a verse.

"Read this, Dave. Aloud."

Dave read: " 'In Him is life and the life is the light of men.' Why, that's what your little leaflet said."

"Yes," said Dr. Barnhart. "Now read this." He pointed farther down.

" 'But as many as received Him to them gave He the power to become the sons of God.' "

"Do you realize that is practically what you have done, Dave? In asking for light you have asked for Him, *the* Son of God. Do you accept Him as your Saviour?"

Dave stared wonderingly. "I can see that I sure need a Saviour," he said.

"Is there any other able to save? Anyone else who gave his life to save you?"

"N—no," answered Dave thoughtfully.

"Then will you take Him now?"

Dave drew a long painful breath.

"I'd like to, sir, but I don't know how."

"Just tell Him so. It's as simple as that. He's God. He hears you."

Dave's head went down, lower and lower. Twice he tried to speak and his voice choked. The doctor waited. The third time Dave drew another long stammering breath and seemed to let go.

"Oh, Christ!" he said, "I know I need You. I'll take You now for my Saviour." He gave a quick sobbing gasp and looked up.

The doctor smiled approval as if he felt that Dave had just done the most sensible thing in the world.

"Now read your verse again. Do you see what it says? What are you now?"

Dave looked puzzled.

"Read it again."

Dave read: " 'As many as received Him, to them gave He the power to become the sons of God.' "

"What are you, according to that?"

"It seems wrong to say such a thing, but it says I'm a son of God."

"It isn't wrong, Dave! It's right, to say what God says is true. The wrong is *not* to say it, not to receive Him." The doctor turned over a few leaves. "Now read this."

Dave read eagerly: "He that believeth on the Son hath everlasting life."

"What do you have, Dave?"

The boy's eyes widened in wonder. "It *says,* 'everlasting life.'"

"Exactly. Do you *feel* that you have it?"

"N—no."

"Then how do you know you do?"

"Well, it says so there. That's supposed to be God's Book, isn't it?"

"That's right, Dave. Stick to it! Some morning you will wake up and you'll feel horrible, and discouraged, and the devil will tell you it's all nonsense, that you imagined all this. But remember you don't go by your feelings. You go by the Word of God."

Dave took a deep breath again and nodded as if relieved.

"Now I'm going to give you some directions. You've just been born into the family of God. What's the first thing a baby does?"

Dave hesitated. "Why, sir, I've had very little to do with babies." He grinned sheepishly.

"Well, I'll tell you. It yells." They both laughed. "Now, you do the same! Go and make yourself heard. I mean, tell somebody what He has done for you. The next thing a baby needs is food. And here's your food, Dave. Take this book— I brought you a Bible in case you didn't have one. Read it every day. Chew it. Digest it.

"Then there's one more thing a baby needs. No, you wouldn't know. Love! A baby doesn't thrive without it. Find some other Christians and spend time with them. I can help you there, perhaps. But first, tell somebody right away about what He has done for you. Do you see how to grow?"

Dave looked wonderingly at his new friend. "I guess so. It's all so new to me."

"The Lord will lead you, and make it plain step by step. Now I have to hurry off."

"Wait," said Dave. "Is Dad worse?"

"No, there's no change. I don't expect it yet. No, I just came over to see you and get better acquainted."

Dave looked at him in astonishment.

"You mean you came all the way up here just for me?" he said incredulously.

"Why certainly, I often have urgent calls when a baby is due, and—" his eyes sparkled with fun, "I figured you were about to arrive. I got here just in time, didn't I? The Lord is able to bring His own sons into life without me, I know that. But I'm glad to have had some little part in it. It's the most thrilling thing in the world."

Dave was still gazing in awe over the fact that a man cared so much about him.

"Do you know, Doctor, this is the first time in my life anybody ever came just to see me? I can't get over it."

"Well, bless your heart, son, it won't be the last time I climb this hill. I hope there will be many times of fellowship. I can't always stay very long, there are so many calling for help, but perhaps sometime you will go with me on my calls."

"That would be wonderful, sir. I'd like that, very much."

"We'll do that. How about Sunday? I'll have a lot of calls, and an operation or two. If you'd care to watch, I'll get you in."

"I sure would, sir. I've always been interested in doctoring. Used to think I'd be a surgeon some day."

Dr. Barnhart smiled. "There is more than one kind of surgery, son. We'll talk about it. Now let's just have a word with the Lord together."

The doctor bowed his head right there in the hall and in a loving way that brought tears to Dave's eyes he prayed for him and his father too and asked for his salvation. Dave shook his head.

"That'll be the day," he grinned incredulously. "If you ever get my father to listen. But thank you again, Doctor," said Dave earnestly, "for the Book, and for—everything."

"It was a pleasure. We'll both pray for your father. You'll see how God works. Good night, Dave."

He went whistling off down to his car.

In wonder and amazement Dave turned into bed and slept as he had not slept since he was a baby.

He even forgot about Darla. But Darla was at that very moment writing a note to Dave.

Darla had not been as indifferent to the broken date as she seemed to be when she marched off from under Dave's eyes with the colonel. It was only that more important things might be accomplished through the officer. She felt she could count on patching things up with Dave and make another date with him, but the colonel was a bigger fish. She had not expected him and his coming had caused her plans to go awry. But she was used to seizing opportunities and making the most of them. Now it was time to make up with Dave.

Darling Dave:

You just can't know how disappointed I was when seven o'clock came Thursday evening and you weren't there. I had really counted on our trip together, and when you didn't come and didn't come, I admit I was a little hurt. Then the tiresome old colonel turned up—I have to be nice to him, he's a friend of my uncle—and I agreed to go out with him. I didn't enjoy the evening one bit. But I do think I covered up pretty well, don't you? I don't believe he suspected when you came, how much I would rather have gone with you.

Now are you going to forgive me for not waiting just one little minute longer for you? If you will, please try me again. Come over Tuesday evening and we'll make a date to go to the plant. Then we can have dinner together as we had planned. I really need to see you. You've been *so* good to me. I need your help again about the accident insurance. The man was here again today asking more questions.

I'll be looking for you Tuesday.

Your disappointed
DARLA.

Darla read over the note, and gave an impish giggle when she came to the part about the colonel being a friend of her uncle.

"My dear, dear Uncle Sam. If he only knew!" she murmured enigmatically. Then she folded the note and addressed it with her characteristic flourish. "Well, it's a great life. Never a dull moment."

Then she kicked off her furry mules and threw her filmy negligee over a chair and slid into bed. But her thoughts were still whirling and she did not immediately drop off to sleep. There were wires to be pulled and knotty threads to be untangled. She lay a long time staring up at the dim ceiling where shadows lurked, for she never darkened her room entirely. The intermittent hum of traffic eleven floors below seemed to keep in rhythm to the scheming wheels incessantly spinning in her brain. Once she suddenly seized her covers and buried her head in them suppressing a smothered cry, as of terror. But she soon snatched them down again and began to breathe deep and fast. At last, worn out apparently with the effort of meshing all the gears in her mind, she fell asleep.

CHAPTER XIII

DAVE AWOKE Saturday morning with a pleasant sense of eagerness. He found that he was actually looking forward to the ride with Davey. Except for the date with Darla that had exploded in his face, as it were, he had not had anything special to look forward to after work for a long time. He occasionally went to a twilight ball game, even played sometimes himself, but usually he was tired and discouraged and ball games didn't take away that feeling. He often wondered if it wasn't people, not things nor even happenings, that made the difference between peace and discontent.

But this morning everything was different. Something, whatever it was that had taken place last night, was still real. The light had not faded. None of his circumstances had changed, but something inside of him certainly had. He was aware of an eagerness, too, to read more in that Bible Dr. Barnhart had given him, to find out more about the wonderful change, to get better acquainted with the wonderful Person who had made the change. Dave had never before thought of Christ as real. Now he was strangely aware of not being alone. There was nothing eerie or uncanny about it, but he knew that a personality was with him, another Somebody, who cared. He had never experienced anything like this in all his life, nor dreamed of such a thing.

As he got together his solitary breakfast he was no longer possessed by the despondency that had been growing upon him for years. He realized that he was looking forward to things, to people, to meeting that doctor again and going with him Sunday, to being with the boy Davey and enjoying the child's pleasure. He wanted to see his eyes light up and hear the chirp of joy in his voice as he saw again the wonders of spring in the country. A few days ago Dave wouldn't have cared particularly. Now everything was fresh and enticing.

He sat down to his toast and eggs and suddenly realized how good it was that he was able to get these things. He had never in all his life had to go without a meal. He bowed his head and wordlessly gave thanks to the One whom he saw now had cared for him all along. Why? He didn't know. Certainly it was not because of any good in himself. He had never committed any crimes, yet for the first time in his life he began vaguely to realize that sin was manifest in attitudes, not acts alone. This magnificent Person whom he had just met who was constantly with him now, he had neglected and insulted for years, voluntarily though not always consciously. He kept wanting to apologize to Him. How gracious He had been not to cast him off long ago.

For the first time since he could remember, Dave had an impulse to whistle or sing as he started downstairs to go to work. He didn't know anything to whistle and he had never sung much. But he snatched at an old scrap of a song he had heard somewhere on the radio and managed a cheery sound that must have surprised the birds. Even Uncle Harry, hearing it from his lonely breakfast table in the enormous dirty kitchen put down his slopping coffee cup and looked out. Malice and envy crept into his eyes. What did that boy have to whistle about? Worthless, chiseling son of a hateful, chiseling father! Once again Uncle Harry fell to counting up the sum of money which might have been to the credit of the

Mathers' account if Jason Truscott and his son had paid the share of expenses that he felt they should have paid all these years. He had done this so often that the figure had grown now to quite a sizable amount. Of course it was always based on Uncle Harry's own estimate of what such payments should have been.

The old man made an ugly noise of contempt as Dave's car chugged out of the driveway. What right had Dave to a car? By rights he and Amelia should have the money Dave had spent on it. In that sense, it was really the Mathers' car. Of course, Amelia had bought a car herself, an old model, and it was standing out on their side of the house now. But she had never let Harry drive it. He had never made the effort to learn how to drive. Still, he resented it that Dave did not offer to take his uncle into town to see how his wife was. It was a long walk down the hill to the bus for a man troubled with arthritis.

But Dave was oblivious of the bitter thoughts that followed him this morning. He was planning where he would take the Wrenns for a drive.

He worked with an interest that he had not had for some time. More than one of the men noticed it and made comment. Dave wanted to tell them what had happened, but he hardly knew how to bring it up, or what to say. Perhaps an opportunity would come later when he had learned a little more himself.

He had slipped the Bible into his coat pocket and today instead of lounging with the rest at lunch as he sometimes did on Saturdays for want of any other place to go, he took off in his car and found a quiet spot overlooking a sunny meadow and began to read as he ate.

He started in at Genesis and soon became so fascinated

that when he suddenly looked at his watch he was astonished. It was past time to go for the Wrenns.

When he arrived at the Pearl Street house Davey was dressed and ready and so excited he could hardly contain himself. Dave carried him down and they made him comfortable in the back seat with his feet up. Anne sat in front and turned sideways so that she could reach to tuck him up if he needed her.

"What would you like to see first, the airport?" asked Dave turning to little Davey before they started.

"Oh *yes!*" cried the boy fervently.

Dave and Anne exchanged an understanding smile over his eagerness, and off they went.

They had gone only a few blocks when Davey called to his friend.

"Are you *very* glad to be taking us for a ride today, Big Dave?"

"Surely I am," responded Dave. "Why?"

"Well, I just wondered. I never saw you like this. You seem different somehow. Not nearly so—so *middle-aged* as you used to."

"Davey!" cried Anne rebukingly, though she couldn't help joining in Dave's roar of laughter.

"I guess I have been pretty much of an old grouch, Davey," he admitted. "You're right, I am different. I am ashamed that you had to prod me to tell you, for I was planning to, but I just don't know how to say it. I guess you will understand, though. Last night I—" he paused and hesitated for words while Anne and Davey waited breathlessly, "I took Jesus Christ as my Saviour, Davey, and everything's different."

"Oh boy, oh *boy!*" cried Davey ecstatically. "Now you'll

really be like one of the family. I've been asking God to make you, and He did. Boy, oh boy!"

A little embarrassed pause crept between them all for a moment. Dave wondered at the new thrill that made him want to shout for joy, since he had told them of his new Saviour. He stole a glance at Anne and saw that her cheeks were pink with delight and her eyes were sparkling. She half turned to him and said shyly,

"We're both very glad, 'Big Dave.' There's nothing like knowing the Lord."

"I'm beginning to believe that," said Dave eagerly. "I'm pretty new at it yet. The man that showed me the way says I'm just a baby and I've got to grow. But so far it's wonderful. I don't remember ever being really happy before in my life."

Anne stole another look at him. The downward lines of his face were turned up this morning, and the bitterness was fading but she could still see the marks that sorrow had left and she wondered, but she would not ask him. Some day he might tell, and it would do him good.

Davey was quiet, too, trying to imagine what it must be like not to be happy.

Then they crossed the bridge and came upon the airport. Great silver wings were flashing here and there, rising, dipping, landing, and soaring again. It was like an enormous bird sanctuary. Davey gasped with pleasure.

"Oh, can't we park here and watch awhile?" he begged.

"I figured you would want to," laughed Dave drawing up as near the airstrip as possible. "Maybe you would like to go over there by the fence where you can see them better?" He opened the back door and took the delighted boy in his arms and together they all sauntered up and down watching one and another of the multitude of great ships swoop and land, rev up and take off, till Davey gave a great sigh of joy and hugged Dave tightly around his neck.

"I never thought I'd see anything like this!" he said, with tears of joy in his voice.

"Someday maybe you'll have a ride in one," suggested Dave. "You never know what wonderful things may happen." He wondered at himself as he said it. It was not what he would have said or even thought a few days or even twenty-four hours ago. But he knew it was true.

Dave pointed out the numerous commercial planes and told of the foreign countries they would soon be visiting.

Then they went back to the car before Davey should get too tired. They drove around the basin where the cherry trees were just beginning to show their new spring ruffles.

Then Davey asked to see the plant where Dave worked. So they crossed the river and started down the east side, past the Naval Air Station where Davey had to stop again and watch the planes. He marveled at the way they flew in close formation, and held his breath thinking every minute there would be a crackup or that one would at least clip another's wing. He was thrilled to see them break their nines into threes and their threes into singles that soared and then whined to a gentle stop, one at a time.

They parked quite awhile there and Anne began to ask about the country around.

"Are there mostly farms or big estates out here?" she wanted to know. "I keep wondering whether there isn't some place where Davey could go for the summer. The doctor has said so often that if only he could be outdoors most of the time he would improve much faster. Yet that's impossible where we are and I don't see how I can afford to make a

change. If only there were some place where I could get work
after school is out, I'd do anything. I'd even do housework
or take in washing if it would get Davey out of the city. But
I hardly know where to start looking. I don't know a soul
outside the city, and I guess Davey has told you we are the
only ones left of our family now. I've no uncles or cousins or
aunts to help. I've asked casually among the schoolteachers,
but none of them seem to know of anything I could do. I
even asked for a job in summer school but they are all taken.
Anyway, even if I could earn enough to send Davey to the
country, I'd still have to pay my own board. And besides,
there would be nobody to give Davey his leg treatments. I
just don't know how it is going to work out. I know the
Lord has a way, though." She smiled bravely.

While she spoke, Dave looked intently at her, for she was
not noticing him. She was staring off at the countryside. He
studied her firm sweet lips, the tired lines about her eyes, he
took in the shabbiness of her old black suit and the capable
look of her hands as they lay restlessly clasping and unclasp-
ing in her lap.

Three times he opened his mouth to speak and then shook
his head. Finally he said, hesitatingly,

"I know of a place where they *very much* need help, but I
don't suppose you would want to do it. It would be grueling
work, and almost no pay, I'm afraid, except board and room."

He expected her to shake her head that that wouldn't do,
but instead she grasped at it.

"Do you really? Oh, I'd take *any*thing, just to get Davey
out in this air and sunshine, and be near him. Would they let
me have him with me, do you suppose?"

"Yes, I'm sure they would. In fact, they would be delighted to have Davey." He tossed a smile back at the boy who was listening alertly now with big wondering eyes.

"Really? Do you know them?" asked Anne.

"Yes, I know them," replied Dave. "All too well I know them!" he added sourly. "It's a horrible place. You wouldn't like it, I'm quite sure." Dave was aghast at himself now for having made the suggestion. He had only half meant it at first. But the more he thought of it the more wonderful he felt it would be—for his family. But he couldn't imagine the gentle, gracious, immaculate Anne Wrenn struggling with the shiftlessness of his family in the big old house.

"What difference would it make whether I like it or not?" cried Anne. "If it's a place the Lord has planned for me and it will help Davey, that's all that matters. Where is it? I don't care how hard the work is, if I can do it."

Dave turned and gazed squarely into Anne's face, seriously studying her. She looked back as frankly without wavering.

At last he said, "I believe you mean that."

"I certainly do." She smiled. "I'd be delighted."

"All right," he said shutting his lips in a determined line. "You've asked for it. I'll take you there."

He started his car and drove on past Bolling Field where Davey squealed with delight again, past the Naval Research laboratory, which he pointed out carelessly as "the place where I work" to the adoring Davey, and a mile beyond, where he turned off the main road onto a third-rate gravel road that led steeply up, winding through pine trees to the top of the hill. Anne caught her breath with the beauty of the distant view but Dave said hoarsely,

"Wait till you see the *dump* at the top."

They turned in between the old stone gateposts and there

in plain view was the big, dark, old pile, in all her dilapidated majesty.

The afternoon sun had chosen that moment to point a flaming finger at the very window where the paper was stuffed in the hole, and its shutter still hung at a crazy angle. One of Uncle Harry's hens strutted across the rickety porch and slowly descended the steps, squawking resentment at the guests, as if hens and not humans were the hosts of the house.

Last week's dirty scrub rags still dangled from Aunt Amelia's sagging clothesline. They were weathered now, showing how long it was between cleanings in that house.

There wasn't a sign of life. Uncle Harry had probably got himself together at last and gone in to see his wife. Never had the place looked so hopelessly dreary to Dave. It was all he could do to choke back his shame and dismay to think that he had had the effrontery to imagine that anyone would be willing to come to such a place and spend a whole summer.

It was a long minute before he dared to look up at Anne's face lest he see the scornful expression there.

But when he did he found she wasn't looking at the house at all. Her eyes were fastened on the far horizon, his own sunset place that she had already discovered, and there was a look of eagerness and wonder upon her face.

At last she turned to Dave, her eyes alight.

"Do you mean that you think I could get work *here,* in this gorgeous spot?"

Dave gaped.

"Gorgeous?" he gulped. "What do you see gorgeous about it? It's nothing but a godforsaken *dump.*"

"Oh, the house needs a little fixing, but all this space," she cried, "and the view! It's marvelous. If I thought Davey could be out here this summer, I'd cry for joy!"

Dave simply stared.

"Well!" he gave forth at last. "I guess things are all in the way you look at them."

She laughed. "Tell me more."

He took a deep breath.

"Okay. Here goes. I may as well give with the whole tale. This, Miss Wrenn, is where I've lived, as long as I can remember."

He glanced at her to see how she'd take that. All he noted was a sudden softening of her face.

She was thinking that already she could understand better those lines of bitterness around his mouth.

Davey had been very quiet for some time, trying to take in the wonderful thought of being out here. He was listening to every word.

"But that's not the half of it. My mother left us years ago because my father was so impossible. No, I know what you're thinking. He didn't drink, but he might as well have. He wouldn't keep a job, and finally gave up trying for one. He was a bear, and still is. My mother died seven years ago. This house belongs to my father and his sister and they used to fight like cats. Now they don't speak. She is married to a —maybe I shouldn't say this, but you may as well know the worst—a man who is a complete zero. All he knows is how to be mean. There was a chance to sell this place ten years ago but my father and aunt couldn't agree and they lost the opportunity. Then prices went down. Dad has had three strokes and he had another just Thursday night. Aunt Amelia is in the hospital with a broken leg. They will probably both be home before long and I can't afford to hire one nurse, let alone two. That's the picture. I don't know why I told you, or ever had the brass to bring you out here."

Dave's face was flushed and his eyes bored hard into the distance. When he began he had scarcely been able to get the words out, but once started he poured out the whole story as if he were glad to get it told and done with.

He waited for Anne's verdict. Of course no girl in her right mind would want to undertake a job like that in a place like this. He dreaded lest she sympathize with him. He could stand anything but that.

But when she spoke she didn't even mention him.

"Oh, just think how wonderfully God could change all that bitterness," she cried. "And what a lovely place this could be with just a little care. I'd *love* to try it. It just needs a good cleaning up—its face washed and its hair combed. A little paint on the trim would practically give it a new dress. And flowers! Think what zinnias and marigolds and petunias would do for it. Why there's no end to what we could do!"

Dave looked at her in astonishment. "Are you crazy?" he said.

"Well, possibly," she answered. Was that twinkle in her eyes trying to hide tears? He wasn't sure. But at least she wasn't sentimentally sorry for him, and she didn't mind the dump. He laughed with relief.

"Why?" she prodded. "Can't you see how a little fixing would do wonders?"

He frowned and shook his head. "Frankly, no. But I guess I never tried. It always seemed like a rotten deal to me. But somehow everything looks different today."

"Did it ever occur to you," she said gently, "that the Lord sometimes allows all of us to get to the end of our rope, so that we will be helpless enough to call on Him? I've had to get there more than once. It sure hurts. But it's worth it."

"I see that now," said Dave, lifting his eyes from the dark

cave beneath the dashboard to the pine-trimmed horizon. "I was blind before. In the dark."

They were silent awhile, understanding each other.

Dave stole a look at her. Her glance seemed to rest lovingly on each part of the old place he had hated so long, as if she were seeing visions. She began to describe how it would look when they finished. Even Dave caught a little of her enthusiasm and allowed his imagination to share in her planning.

At last they thought to turn and see what Davey was doing. He was sound asleep on the back seat, a healthy pink flush on his cheeks that Anne hadn't seen in months.

"You don't know how grateful I am for this ride," she said softly. "And for the chance to come out here and help."

"You don't really mean it, do you?" asked Dave with wonder. "Your patients will be completely ornery, I can promise you that."

"The Lord will have to give me grace for that part," she laughed. "But I haven't found anything yet He can't do, if we're willing. That's the catch. Sometimes we think we are when we're not. We try to tell Him *how* He must work and He won't have us dictating that way. But in this case I'm really more than glad to take the offer. Who will it be who has the right to—shall I say 'hire 'n fire' me?"

Dave chuckled. "I guess it's yours truly. I'm getting you for Dad and I'll be providing what food there is. Aunt Amelia will undoubtedly have to have somebody, and when she finds she can get a nurse cheap, she'll go for you. Maybe she'll fork over and maybe she won't. You mustn't let her run over you, though. She'll extract every bit of energy you have, making demands. You will just have to set your limits and stick to them. Dad is grouchy, but he's not as bad as that."

Anne raised her pretty, determined chin. "I guess she won't be harder to manage than forty sixth-graders," she laughed.

"Well, is it a deal?" asked Dave, slow to believe his good fortune.

"It's a deal," Anne responded gaily. "When do I start? School's out a week from Friday."

"I'll let you know. It won't likely be before then, anyway. Remember I haven't mentioned money yet," he warned.

"I'll not worry about that," said Anne. "You will have to feed me or I can't do your work," she giggled. "And if you don't feed Davey, I'll leave, so there!"

"I guess I'm on the spot then," agreed Dave with another chuckle. "Well, I feel a lot better already. Dr. Barnhart said the Lord would work out the problems once I let go. He sure does!"

They wound their way down the hill and back to Pearl Street, silent most of the way, thinking. Dave was overcome with wonder over the marvelously simple solution to his problem, and Anne was busy planning how she could bring cheer to the old place on the hill.

Chapter XIV

Dave was up and out early Sunday morning. Dr. Barnhart lived in the village at the foot of the hill, and he left on his calls at eight.

He found the house, a low, wide, hospitable-looking place, and parked outside till the doctor should be ready. He had slipped his new Bible into his pocket to be handy in case he had long waits here and there on the rounds. He was already deep into Genesis again when he heard the joyous whistle and saw the doctor come smiling out. What a man! He acted as if he never had a care in the world himself. Dave wondered what his family life was like.

"Well, I see you've got a good appetite already, Dave," remarked the doctor glancing at the Bible.

"I sure have. It tastes good, too. I can't thank you enough, Doctor. By the way, I never knew there were footnotes in the Bible. They certainly help to make it clear."

"They are not a part of the text, of course," explained the doctor, "but they do help. It would take years of study to get for yourself what is in them. I selected that special 'Pilgrim' edition because its notes are geared for beginners."

"I'm a beginner, all right," laughed Dave. "It's all brand-new to me. For instance, I never knew before all that about the original creation being destroyed so many millions of years ago. I always supposed that the Bible didn't know any better than that creation began with Adam. That's what they

151

gave us to understand in school and that was one of the main reasons, they said, for disbelieving it."

"That's what is generally given out, partly because people don't know any better. But why *don't* they know better? Isn't it because they don't want to, or don't care enough to find out? The apostle Paul says it's because they won't receive the '*love* of the truth.'"

"I never had any particular love of the truth," said Dave.

"You think you didn't? I never saw anybody latch on to the truth much faster than you did. But of course, He says you were 'chosen in Him before the foundation of the world.'"

"That's too deep for me. I don't get it."

"Of course not. Nobody does. But God says it. Don't try to understand God's foreknowledge and man's free will, Dave. You never will. Lots of people stumble over that and never get any farther. Just accept them both. If you could understand all God says and does He wouldn't be any greater than you are. You wouldn't want a *little* God to worship, would you?"

"I reckon not. But it's all so new."

"That's right. And you'll never get to the end of God's wonders."

"Yes, I believe that now. I didn't used to. I thought He must have made a mistake, or else He didn't care. I see things so differently now."

"You have things in the right order now."

"What do you mean?"

"God never said, 'See and then believe.' He always says, 'Believe, and then I'll let you see.'"

"I never thought of that," said Dave and he was quiet again.

It was a fascinating day for the boy. They visited all sorts of places and each time the doctor would have some anecdote or life story to tell. Betweentimes Dave was asking questions about the Bible. As he read during the doctor's calls he was always ready with a new problem. He was astonished at the doctor's deep knowledge of the Book.

When dinnertime came they had worked their way back to the home village and Dr. Barnhart said,

"Now you're coming in and have a bite with us. I want you to meet my family."

It felt good to be invited to a real home meal and not have to be thinking all the time of what people would say if they knew how he lived. The doctor knew and didn't let it bother him. Dave relaxed and enjoyed himself.

Mrs. Barnhart was small and plump with lots of firm flesh that made dimples in unexpected places. She loved to laugh and, as Dave told her, she was a wonderful cook. She seemed pleased at his compliment and told him to drop in again any time.

The afternoon was spent at the hospital. The doctor took him in to see an appendectomy and two or three minor operations.

Dave watched the surgeon's preparations for an appendectomy with amazement. He had never dreamed of such ceremony.

"I felt like a germ-covered monster," he told the doctor afterward, "when I saw you and the rest washing, and washing and washing."

The doctor smiled. "Wait till you get to the book of Leviticus. You won't be surprised."

"The book of Leviticus, what has that to do with it?"

Dave asked. He never knew what this man would bring up next.

"Leviticus gives God's rules for Jewish priests. God required the priests to wash before every service they did for Him, did you know that?"

"Good night, no! What for?"

"To teach them how much He hates uncleanness. We doctors have to make certain that we are absolutely spotless before we use the scalpel on a human body, but it's a lot more important for a servant of God who uses the Word of God on human souls to have everything in his life clean. Don't you see how God has made all the physical things to be a picture of spiritual things?"

Dave was bewildered.

"The sword of the Spirit," explained the doctor, "is a name for the Word of God when God uses it on His enemies. But He says it's sharper and keener than a sword when He has to operate on us with it. You might say it's like a scalpel. You know, I used His Word like that on you the other night?"

Dave nodded. "Yes, it went deep, too."

"Well, suppose there was something in my life that was not right. For instance, suppose you should later discover that I was cheating somebody, or mistreating my wife, or nursing a grievance or an unforgiving spirit. Don't you see how that uncleanness in me would get into you, just like germs on a surgeon's hands might cause infection in the patient? I mean, you would notice it and it would bother you. Some sin like that might hinder God's work in you and you wouldn't become the strong healthy 'baby' you are. Now I don't mean I'm perfect by any means, but I can't let any known sin remain in my life if I expect God to use me. Don't you see?"

Dave agreed. But this thing was beginning to go too deep for comfort. Somehow the thought of Aunt Amelia and Uncle Harry kept bothering him. It had never occurred to him before that his feeling about them might be called sin. He was sure that it was impossible to feel any other way about them. He was astonished that he resented the thought of giving up that feeling. Did he actually *enjoy* hating them? That seemed rather horrible. It wasn't any of it pleasant to think about. He was glad when the doctor drew up in front of a small frame building.

"I generally try to get in at least part of a church service Sundays," said Dr. Barnhart.

The singing had already begun when they entered.

"That's Dr. Barnhart," loudly whispered a smiling, wheezy old lady in front of them to her neighbor. "Got a heart as big as a barn too." They both nodded enthusiastically.

Dave grinned at the doctor, who looked sheepish.

The sermon was short. It was the story in the book of Esther about the king who had forgotten to reward a certain servant for saving his life until one night when he couldn't sleep. He demanded to have the state records brought and he discovered what he had done and made it right.

"I'm convinced," said the preacher, "that many a time when we can't sleep it's because God has something to say to us that we're too busy to listen to in the daytime."

Dave shrugged off the moral. He was never troubled with sleeplessness. He scarcely knew what it was.

After the service the doctor introduced him to the pastor

and several friends, "almost as if I were his own son," thought Dave with pleasure.

He was very happy when finally he said good-bye to Dr. Barnhart, took his own car, and started up the hill. His lights outlined the figure of a man a little way ahead, who was painfully picking his way among the loose stones of the road. It was Uncle Harry. Ordinarily Dave would have whizzed by, letting Uncle Harry make his own way to the top, but this time something made him stop. He reached over and opened the door on his uncle's side.

"Get in, Uncle Harry," he said pleasantly. "I'll take you up." It was surprising how righteous the small favor made him feel.

His uncle stared at him. Then grumpily he gave a snort of assent and climbed in. But not a word did he say all the way up to the house. The old hatred rose up and Dave wondered whether such a feeling as this could ever be cleansed from him. Surely even God Himself must be disgusted with this man! There was no use in trying to be nice to him. He let him out at the back porch before driving on around to the porte-cochere. But a depression settled upon him. How glad he was that the house was large!

Dave dropped off to sleep quickly, but some time in the night he awoke with a start.

He thought he had heard Uncle Harry calling him. He waited. There was no sound. He had better try answering.

"Yes?" he called. No answer.

What if Uncle Harry had had a stroke or were sick or something? Well, it would serve him right if he had. Let him lie and take it. Dave certainly didn't owe him any kindness.

Then as plainly as if his doctor friend were there Dave

seemed to hear him say, "Suppose God had said that about you?"

Then it began, an argument with himself that lasted for two or three hours. He turned and he tossed and each direction he faced there was another ugly fact about his hatred for Uncle Harry, staring right at him. He dragged out as alibis one mean thing after another that Uncle Harry had done, but not even all of them together seemed large enough to quench that great burning fire of malice in his own heart.

Sunday morning he had had some idea of letting the Lord use him as He did Dr. Barnhart, but now he saw that his hands were not clean. He wasn't fit to be used.

After a long time what Anne had said came back to him: "I haven't found anything He can't do if we're willing, that's the catch."

And he knew that it was. To love that man whom he hated was beyond his own power, and he wasn't willing to let God do it. That's what it amounted to.

At last he crawled out of bed and got down on his knees. "Oh God," he said aloud. "I'm a *stinker*. I can't love Uncle Harry. If he's got to be loved, You will have to do something about it."

And then he crept back and went to sleep.

But Dave slept late and had to hurry in the morning. He didn't even have time for any reading in his Bible, and his prayer was hasty. Something was definitely wrong but he didn't have time to stop and find out what it could be.

Things didn't go well at the plant either. He had thought he would start the day by telling somebody how he had found the Lord, but the words just wouldn't come. Perhaps he had better wait again. He was obsessed, too, with worry over how the others in the house would feel about having Anne and

Davey there. Maybe they would say he had had no business
to make plans for them. But somebody must. And if he was
going to make himself responsible for the Wrenns' support
while they were there, surely nobody could object. It was the
cheapest way out that he could see.

That was another thing. He didn't feel right about not paying Anne something. And yet just the food for her and
Davey would strain his pay check. He thought of selling his
beloved car and getting a bicycle to go to work. He could
even walk. It wasn't so very far. But that would mean that
none of them would ever get off the place. And how could he
get groceries? Perhaps one of the stores in the village would
deliver. The problems kept going the rounds all day. He
didn't seem to be any better off than he had been last week.
What was the matter?

When he reached home he stopped at the mailbox as a matter of course just before he drove in the gate. There was
rarely any mail. Occasionally an electric-light bill, but it
wasn't time for that. Anyway, Aunt Amelia always paid that
and he gave her a certain percentage of it. That was one of
the bones of contention. Uncle Harry always said he didn't
pay enough.

He flipped the box open and there was a letter. It was a
square envelope, not like a bill. The paper was fine and
creamy. It was addressed to him. Astonished, he hurried up
the drive and parked.

He didn't wait to get out of the car. He turned the letter
over and opened it. An ever so faint scent of Oriental per-
fume wafted from it. Then he saw the handsome monogram,
D R D and his heart turned over.

He read the letter again and again until he knew every
word and every flourish. He thought he had never seen such

beautiful handwriting. Surely, he thought, God was good to him. "Darling Dave." Such joy as this he had not dreamed of. He went upstairs and started supper in a daze.

Soon he would be seeing Darla again!

Chapter XV

Her problems on the way to solution, Anne recovered strength and went back to school Monday with a light heart, although she was utterly exhausted at the end of each day's work.

The insurance company informed her that they were making an adjustment with Darla's company and a check would soon be on its way to her for the full amount of damage to her car, the hospital bills and reimbursement for her days of absence from work. She was astonished and grateful. She had not realized that all that could come about without her making any attempt to fight for it.

Dave stopped in early on Tuesday evening to see whether she wouldn't like to go out to the house again Saturday and plan how she would like things arranged. She noticed that he was dressed up and looked very slick and polished. He seemed to be in a hurry, excited and very much preoccupied.

Davey was disappointed that he couldn't stay and Anne felt a little troubled after he left. The shine of his face that he had had last Saturday was not so evident. She did hope that his experience with the Lord had not been a mere superficial emotional spree that would wear off. He had appeared to be so sincere. She began to pray for him quietly in her heart.

But Dave was eagerly making his way to Darla's apartment. He was not aware that he needed prayers. He was too excited. This would be a real get-acquainted visit with Darla.

She had asked for it. She would be really herself, at home, and perhaps he would meet her family and learn more of her background. He could not yet imagine telling her all about himself, but perhaps after tonight, when he knew her better, he would feel so close to her that he could. He did have an idea that he would like to tell her about his new life in the Lord. He was not sure how she would take it. Would she laugh? That slow mocking laugh of hers could stab terribly. It seemed to set him miles away from her. But perhaps he would find that she was already a Christian. He was too new in the ways of the Lord yet to discern. That all-night party she had been to with the colonel—well, she had said she didn't enjoy it! Perhaps that was because she knew it wasn't the sort of thing for a Christian to do. By the time he reached Rock Creek, he had just about persuaded himself that Darla wore a halo.

His hand fairly trembled with excitement as he knocked. He expected the door to open and he would see her at last, but instead he heard her voice calling,

"Come in, David." Nobody else ever called him David. The name seemed beautiful when she spoke it.

He opened the door and walked in.

To him it seemed like an enchanted palace, with its soft deep rugs thrown over the carpet hushing every step, its bewildering mirrors, its lifelike ivory statuettes, nude nymphs, poised as if about to come to life like genii and warn him perhaps of fearful dangers he must meet and conquer before he could approach the lovely lady held captive there.

His breath came fast. He made a handsome picture, dressed in his dark blue best, freshly shaven, his black waves slick and shining, his dark eyes radiant with eagerness.

Darla, reclining lazily on her chaise longue, smiled. Her

lovely dimple played in and out. Her eyes greeted him with a welcome just for him, he thought. She lifted a graceful white arm from which the soft blue velvet drapery of her negligee fell away. She gave him her hand and he could scarcely let it go.

She breathed a little sigh and said poutingly,

"Sit here beside me, please," and moved over just a little to make room for him to sit facing her on the couch.

A shadow crossed his eagerness.

"You aren't sick, are you?" he asked anxiously.

She suppressed a look of amusement.

"Oh, no," she assured him, then sighed again. "Just so very tired. And—" she passed an exquisite hand over her eyes. "I get so—so very lonely."

Dave was at a loss. He had a desire to gather her in his arms and assure her that she need never be lonely again while he was in the world. But of course that would not do. All he did was murmur sympathetically:

"I know. It's tough." He was in dead earnest. "Are your folks all away?" he asked.

"Yes," she replied sadly. "I don't have much of a family anyway." Then she suddenly brightened. "But let's talk about you. Tell me more about your work. It seems as if it must be so fascinating; to think that you are working right with the marvelous things that really count in the progress of the whole world. Those tiny little 'copters you told me of, that can be folded up and carried by the score in the big planes, I think that is simply marvelous. How on earth do they work?"

Thrilled to think that this delicate, beautiful, little lady should be interested in such things as planes and weapons, Dave rattled on, telling the little he knew. He scarcely thought of what he was saying for watching for that dimple of hers to peek out. And while he talked he became aware that she was casting admiring glances at him, at his hair, and his eyes, his broad shoulders and his hands. The color rushed up in his cheeks and when he realized that, it grew all the worse. He stammered, trying to remember what he had been saying.

She gave a little laugh as if she knew what was going on in his mind and didn't object. With a friendly gesture she laid a hand on his knee while he talked. Then she reached for the intricately carved chain on his tie clasp, a relic of his father's more affluent days, and toyed with it, asking about it with interest. Then she drew a deep happy breath and said, looking modestly down with a becoming little shyness upon her,

"You don't know how nice it is to have someone to talk to." She looked up at him prettily, trustingly.

He answered solemnly.

"You think I don't? I know what you mean. *And how* I know!"

She smiled gratefully, raising her delicate brows ever so little.

"You're a dear boy. *You* understand!"

"I'll always try to understand."

She gave a slow dimpled smile again. The little rubies in her earring swords twinkled enticingly at him. She looked deep into his eyes and held his. Then impulsively she reached up her little jeweled hands and drew his face down to the smooth creaminess of her neck, whispering in his ear, "You're terrific, David."

The fragrant softness of her hair and skin made his head swim. He trembled in the effort to hold himself from seiz-

ing her and covering her with kisses. He dared not move lest
he break the enchanting moment. She was just a sweet trusting young girl and of course she had no idea what a storm
of longing she had stirred up in him. He forced himself to
lie motionless, trembling, drinking in her sweetness.

After a moment she let him go, pushing him from her with
a soft little laugh. Was it the mocking laugh again?

"You're sweet," she said shyly, looking up at him again.
"Oh, but look! There's blood on your cheek. Ugh!" She
turned her head away prettily.

He put up his hand and sure enough, a red smear was on
his face. He wiped it off with the back of his hand and then
reached for his handkerchief.

"Oh, it must have been from my earrings. I'm *so* sorry.
How careless of me!" She said it with a charming little lisp.
It was all he could do not to take her in his arms again.

He wiped his face with the handkerchief and shrugged.

"It's nothing," he said lightly and gave her a look that
meant he would be glad to shed all the blood in his body for
one more touch of her.

She gave a low laugh once more.

"You must go now, David." She lingered over the last syllable of his name caressingly in a way that made him feel as
if she considered him her own. "I have to go out again
tonight."

"But you're so tired!" he objected, hovering over her.
"And you haven't told me anything about your work," he
chided. "Did you say it was writing?"

She waved her hand. "Oh, sometime I'll tell you about it.
Not tonight. Now don't you forget to get permission for us
to tour the plant next week. And do try to let me see what
goes on in the research laboratory. I think that would be

most interesting. Let me know as soon as you can. Thursday night would be good."

He looked troubled.

"You know Thursday is my night school."

"Oh yes, little schoolboy. I forgot. Well, run along, and make it when you can. I'll be waiting to hear from you." She put a little possessive lilt into her last words that rang in his heart as he went down in the elevator. But he didn't hear her mocking laugh after he had gone out.

He didn't know how long he had been there with Darla. Was it a thousand years or only five minutes? He looked at his watch. Only half-past eight. She had said she had to go out again tonight. The night seemed to darken around him as he remembered that others besides himself had a claim upon her. Oh, but that was business. His date was not. What had he done to deserve such a girl? "That's what the doctor would call 'grace,'" he said to himself.

Then like an electric shock came the realization that he had not thought once of his new Saviour the whole time. He had intended to tell her about Him. Where was He? Dave had had no awareness of His presence in that room with Darla. The thought was startling.

What was wrong?

Did God disapprove of a man loving a woman? He thought of the story of Adam and Eve in Genesis. No. God had certainly created man and woman and given one to the other. And even Eve herself could be no more lovely than this girl.

Yet something was wrong somewhere.

Dave drove slowly home. He wished he could talk it over with the doctor. Maybe he would have the answer.

He kept on the gravel road and turned up the hill. The

lights of a car that had been behind him all the way out
from town flashed by. It was just a plain black car, an old
model. He paid no attention to it.

The bleakness of the empty house struck him afresh as he
entered and trudged up the stairs. He felt definitely lonely,
much more so than he used to before he had known the joy
of a constant Presence with him.

He started to take off his good clothes and he noticed the
blood on the back of his hand. He had forgotten the little
scratch. He put his hand up to his face. The blood had dried
on his cheek. He went into the bathroom to wash it off.
Then he saw red on his other cheek and tried to wash it off.
It didn't wash so easily. It was lipstick. A sort of thrill seized
him again and then a wave of something like guilt. But why
should he feel guilty? Perhaps he was getting fanatical since
that doctor had talked about unclean hands. Why did he always feel clean after reading the Bible? The sword of the
Spirit, Dr. Barnhart had called it.

Darla had swords, too. Exquisite little things. One of hers
had cut him. But it hadn't cleansed; he couldn't shake off
the feeling of guilt. After such a wonderful time with Darla,
why shouldn't he be radiantly happy?

Finally he grew so restless that he dropped to his knees
once more and tried to pray.

"Oh, God! Jesus! Saviour! Yes, that's it, I need a Saviour.
I'm too stupid to know what I need to be saved from, but
I'm asking You to handle it. Maybe I'm just getting crazy.
Or fanatical. If there is something wrong in my life, some
sin, show me. I *think* I want to get rid of it. If I don't really,
then *make* me want to. Amen."

He arose feeling that he had done all he knew to make
things right. He took his Bible and read awhile but found he

could not stay awake, so he turned out the lights and went to bed.

He struggled through the next two or three days, going to work, visiting his father and his aunt, coming home, cooking supper, trying to read awhile, going to bed.

His father was improving, but very slowly. The doctor said the main thing for him was quiet. Nothing must disturb him. He could be taken home any time now but it was vital that he have careful nursing. There must be someone around continually to wait upon him.

Dave told Dr. Barnhart about the way things were working out to have Anne and Davey there. The doctor flashed his joyous smile.

"Didn't I tell you that the Lord would work your problems out if you'd let Him run things?" he rejoiced.

Dave smiled and nodded, "Y-yes," but there wasn't the same eagerness, and the doctor noticed the cloud, thinking to himself, "That boy needs help. I must find time to run up again and have a talk with him." But the days passed and there were more sick than usual. The doctor couldn't get away.

Then came Saturday, and time to go for Anne and Davey. They had planned to let Davey lie out in the old hammock while they worked in the house.

"It's good you came," greeted Anne when Dave arrived. "I think Davey would have burst his buttons if he had waited any longer." They laughed. Davey threw his arms about Dave's neck to make his weight as light as he could. Dave could feel his tension. He was strung up with excitement. It was strange to think that a trip to "that old dump," as Dave had always called his home, could possibly mean such pleasure to someone else.

Before they left the rooming house they counted up what furniture Anne had and did some measuring.

"It's not as though there wouldn't be space enough in the house, goodness knows," said Dave ruefully. "That's about all there is."

"Yes, but it won't do any harm to know just how things will fit in," said Anne. "And don't think for a minute that we are going in and spread ourselves around. A little cubbyhole somewhere is all that we are used to and all that we will need. Remember you told me yourself that your aunt and uncle resent letting you use the house and they may feel that way all the more about two strangers."

"I don't think so," Dave said. "They are likely to be more decent to other people than to their own family. And after all, you know, they are getting a lot of nursing for very little. How little, I don't know. I'm going to get as much out of those old tightwads as I can. I've a notion to tell them that you charge a hundred dollars a week and they can pay half."

"Oh, you won't do any such thing," burst out Anne, laughing and looking at him keenly to see whether he was joking or not. "You are saving me money."

"Saving, my eye!" exploded Dave. "You still don't know what you are getting into. That woman, and Dad too, will have you on the run day and night, and there won't be any way I can stop it. Besides that, you'll still have Davey to look out for. Although I think I can help you with those leg treatments. I did quite a bit of massage when I was in high school. Our coach taught me how."

"Wonderful! I admit that sometimes that's the thing that seems just one straw too many for me."

"I'll be glad to take that over," promised Dave. "And I'd

like to have Dr. Barnhart look at Davey, too. Well, here we are," he said as they reached the top of the hill. "But we seem to have visitors. I hope it's not that old skinflint of a minister again. He tried to do us out of the place last week."

There was a black car parked opposite the stone gateposts at such an angle that it was practically impossible for Dave to turn in, or even to drive past. But it was not a new handsome model like the minister's.

"Must be a farmer who doesn't know how to park," grumbled Dave, slowing up.

A man in a plain dark suit got out of the car, and a police officer in uniform appeared from the other side.

Chapter XVI

They approached Dave.

"Is your name David Truscott?"

"Yes sir." Dave looked them squarely in the face, puzzled. "Were you looking for someone?"

"Yes. For you. This your wife?" Anne blushed and Dave looked more bewildered. Davey giggled.

"No," growled Dave. "Are you sure there isn't some mistake?" he asked as they came toward him rather truculently.

"No mistake, I guess," the officer answered. "You're wanted for questioning."

"About what?" asked Dave raising his voice in amazement.

"We'll tell you at headquarters. Come on."

Dave started to object, but realized that he was dealing with the law. He turned to Anne.

"I haven't a notion what all this is about," he apologized. "I'm sorry you are in on it, whatever it is." Then he turned to the officer. "I have a boy here, sir, who can't get out of the car by himself. May I first carry him up to the house?"

The policeman was gruff and blustering, as if determined to make much of his position before the plain-clothes man.

"Come on," he snarled. "We don't want any fast stuff pulled on us."

It was all Dave could do to keep from snarling back at him. Anne looked distressed.

"Well, I can't just leave him here in the road, sir. His sister is not strong enough to carry him."

Then the detective spoke up.

"Let him drive up, Bill. You follow. I'll go with him."

The man climbed into Dave's car beside Anne and they waited while the policeman pulled the black car over to let them by.

Dave hurried up the drive and placed Davey gently in the hammock. As he leaned over him the boy whispered, "We'll be prayin' for you, Big Dave."

"Thanks, brother," returned Dave. "I'll need it. I haven't an idea what this is about." He turned to Anne. "I'm certainly sorry this is upsetting your visit out here. I'm sure there's a mistake and it will soon be straightened out. Will you please go ahead with the plans and just do as you think best until I get back. If I'm later than lunch time, there's food up in the refrigerator. Help yourself."

"Oh, I brought our lunch with us, thank you. We shall be quite all right. I'll get to work."

With a strange premonition of evil, Dave got into the black car and rode off.

Anne watched them with a troubled countenance. She stood so long after they were out of sight that Davey called to her.

"Anne, come here. What's the matter?"

She came over to the hammock.

"Matter enough, I guess, Davey. At least for Big Dave. I don't understand it."

"I know what you're thinking, that Big Dave has done something wrong. But he hasn't, Anne. He just told me so."

"What do you mean, Davey?" she asked gently with a far-away look as if the child couldn't know what he was talking about.

"I mean just now when he put me in the hammock here, I told him we'd be praying for him and he said, 'Thanks, brother—he called me brother, wasn't that nice? Then he said, 'I'll need it. I haven't an idea what this is about.'"

Anne looked hard at Davey.

"He said that, Davey? I hope—"

"You mean you *hope* it's true! Anne!" he rebuked her. "Don't you believe Big Dave?"

"Oh, yes, Davey, but after all, we don't know him very well."

She looked around at the dreary unkempt place. It certainly was typical of a place where unhealthy doings might be carried on. But she wouldn't say that to Davey. The day that had seemed to promise such pleasure had been very quickly clouded over. What should she do? Take Davey somehow and get out of here? Dave's car was there. She had her driver's license but she was not an experienced driver. Anyway, that would almost amount to stealing his car. If she couldn't trust him she certainly couldn't feel she had a right to his car to get away from him.

There was no other possible method of escape, if she wanted to escape. To carry Davey was out of the question. There wasn't another soul around, as far as she knew. Dave had said he wasn't sure whether Uncle Harry would be there or not. It was Saturday and he might very likely be at the hospital visiting Aunt Amelia. Besides, from all Dave said—if it were true!—Uncle Harry was not the sort of person she would want to appeal to for help. There! She was doubting Dave again. How easy to doubt everything, once a small suspicion crept in.

She desperately wanted to be able to trust Dave. But she felt so uncertain. Police didn't usually apprehend a person for no reason at all.

She went into the strange big empty house and began to reconnoiter. She was a capable girl and she had spent many hours during the last few nights trying to plan how she would be best able to take over the tremendous responsibility that she knew this job would be—*if* it materialized.

She had decided that the more she consolidated, the better and easier her work would be. That if brother and sister were brought together in a situation not of their own planning, it might be that they would be willing to lay down their arms at least for the time being and put up with each other.

She wasn't certain of Uncle Harry. She counted on his being the nonentity Dave had described.

However, the whole matter was going to require as much tact as brawn. Most of the nursing, she figured, would be doing endless little menial errands. That she could manage easily. She would tire, but she was used to being tired.

First she took a look at the downstairs. There was a huge living room, as large as a small bungalow's floor space. It was furnished with what must have been very handsome pieces fifty years ago. Some were handsome still. There were several Oriental rugs that Anne guessed might be valuable.

A spacious hall separated the living room and dining room. Obviously the dining room had once been the heart of the house. There was a roomy bay window there and a worn couch and a sewing machine, besides the big oak dining table and an old-fashioned sideboard. The rug there was worn threadbare. A glass-front china closet, showing exquisite Dresden and Bavarian china sets and a great deal of crystal ware, stood with its door ajar. Dust had settled thick on the dishes.

Not a sound could be heard in the house. It was rather eerie. Anne hesitated before she pushed open the swinging door at the far side of the dining room.

She entered a square room, apparently planned for a breakfast room. It was almost completely filled by a wide, heavy walnut double bed with elaborate carving on head and footboards. The bed showed signs of having been unmade for days. A pair of soiled pajamas lay on the floor where they had been flung off. A curtain suspended by safety pins here and there from a loose string, pretended to form an improvised wardrobe. The curtain was dirty and faded, and most of the garments inside were visible; shabby trousers, a suit, a silk dress or two and a heavy coat. A cracked mirror in a fine antique frame hung above an old bookcase which huddled flat against the one vacant wall. The bookcase held the usual dresser necessities, a comb, some women's things, a crumpled tie. There was barely room to step between it and the bed.

The whole room was a pitiful makeshift. What a way to live, in a big house with all those rooms!

The kitchen would have to be the center of her activities, so she edged her way between the bed and the bookcase and opened the far door. There was a narrow "butler's pantry" with shelves to the ceiling. She crossed it to what must be the kitchen door at last, when all at once she heard a sound, and simultaneously as she flung wide the door into the kitchen, the opposite door from the back porch to the kitchen opened also, and there stood a man with a pipe in his mouth, sagging with surprise.

Uncle Harry stared. It was not his way to react quickly to any stimulus and it seemed a full minute before he slowly put up his hand and took down his pipe. Perhaps he was making it possible for his jaw to drop in amazement without fear of breaking the pipe. At any rate, he opened his mouth, whether to speak or because it wouldn't stay closed. But Anne spoke first.

Smiling her sweetest, she came forward with her hand outstretched.

"Oh, you're Uncle Harry, aren't you?" she exclaimed, as if it were years since she had seen him and he was her favorite uncle.

Uncle Harry swallowed hard. Rivulets of tobacco juice had, through the years, worn gutters down each side of his chin.

He had taken his pipe out with his right hand and he simply wasn't deft enough to effect a change and free his hand to take Anne's. He tried it and got befuddled in his haste and dropped the pipe.

"Oh, I'm sorry," cried Anne with genuine sincerity. She really hadn't meant to cause the accident. Quick as a bird she stooped and picked it up for him, handing it back gracefully. "I'm so glad it didn't break. I suppose I did startle you. You see," she continued to smile while she talked fast, for she realized that much hung upon this first interview, "I didn't know there was anyone around. And I'm quite sure you didn't expect me, did you?" She laughed, a merry, musical laugh, inhibiting the desire to wipe the smell of that pipe off her hand.

"I came out to get my bearings for next Saturday. I'm the nurse, you know, who is to look after the invalids when they come home, and I thought I had better come and find my way around before I plunge into work. What a grand big kitchen."

She chattered on, trying to stall for time hoping to hit upon some subject which would elicit a response from this completely wordless person.

She looked archly up at him, with her most ingratiating smile.

"Would it be asking too much of you to—show me around a little? Or are you busy?" Impishly she added that last, for Dave had told her that the man never lifted a finger.

"That does it!" she whispered to herself.

For the man gave forth with a "Hunh! Hjerupp!" as if clearing his throat, the first sound that he had attempted.

"Why, yes, yes, of course," he assented, and stood perfectly still.

He would have to have further prodding.

She smiled again and looked around the kitchen once more. The very sight of it made her sick, with its unwashed dishes and greasy pans, dirty floor and ants wandering here and there. But that was only dirt; that could easily be scrubbed. This man's soul was a slippery thing to tackle.

"I came in through the dining room," she told him as if to give him a boost, "but I guess a house as large as this has an upstairs and then some."

"Huh. Yes." And then he committed himself in a way that was unprecedented for Uncle Harry. "You ken just go where you like, I reckon. . . . Ain't been nobuddy up there to stop you, fer years, only the old fellow, and he was always an unsociable old devil."

"Well, I'll just look around upstairs then, if I may, and see where we had better fix up a place to nurse your wife.

It's very good of you to let me make myself at home and wander around. I won't be but a few moments, and then I'll be down to ask your opinion, of course, as to what would be best."

That last remark, Anne figured, was taking a long chance. If the man should prove stubborn, it might make things difficult. But she counted on making him think that he had made the decisions. From what Dave said he couldn't decide for himself whether to take the next breath or not. But she believed she could wheedle him into thinking he had planned everything and that would get him on her side. She hoped that wasn't deceitful.

She ran up the stairs, dust flying in her wake, and glanced through the rooms. They seemed innumerable, and so large! It almost seemed as if she might get lost up there. All at once it came to her what a strange and ridiculous situation she was in. She had to stifle a giggle. Here she was, miles from anywhere, in an enormous old house with a perfectly strange old codger, and the good-looking young man who had brought her here was under arrest, or so it seemed, and might never return. She threw a look out at the clean blue sky.

"Oh, Lord," she gasped, "if it weren't for You, I'd be terrified, I suppose. But I do believe You led me here, and here is where I'll stay until You show me the next step. Guide me, and do take care of that nice young man." She whispered the last sentence as if she scarcely could let even God look into her heart.

She whisked around, almost running from room to room, and giving a reticent peek into the couple of rooms that were evidently the premises allowed by the penurious aunt to the brother and nephew. She noted the bare, masculine cleanliness there. It gripped her heart with sympathy and a longing to brighten it up. Her common sense told her that the young man who lived here might be a rascal, even now behind bars. But her heart insisted on believing in him, at least until she knew differently.

After her tour it was plain to her that it would be possible to serve the whole menage only if she had the two invalids downstairs. The little breakfast room would do for Aunt Amelia; she was evidently used to it. But that huge bed would have to go. She would have Dave take it upstairs into one of those big bedrooms for Uncle Harry. He'd probably fuss if he were put out of it entirely.

Mr. Truscott should sleep in the dining room at present, so that she could have him nearer the kitchen and downstairs bath. Later he might not need so much care.

She had discovered a small room off the far side of the dining room which had evidently been used at some time as a conservatory. It was empty and dirty, but it was sunny and could be cleaned. It would make a good enough place for her and Davey. Davey would still need a great deal of care.

She looked at her watch and her heart felt heavy. It was nearly noon.

Where was Dave?

Chapter XVII

Darla was arising at what she considered a very early hour, ten o'clock. According to her frequent custom, she had been out most of the night and she generally slept most of the morning. But she had important business on hand today and she wanted plenty of time to plan it.

She was fixing a leisurely cup of coffee which, with some fruit, was all she allowed her figure for breakfast, when the telephone rang. It seemed to have an urgency about it that made her hasten to it instead of gliding as she generally did.

"Yes?" She had practiced a noncommittal tone. But she was not prepared for what she heard.

In a ghastly whisper Merta Pilchester breathed, "Derau! They've got Dad."

That was all. Instantly Darla sprang into action, a routine she had planned carefully many times.

She was out of her negligee and into her clothes in a flash. She grabbed a ready-packed handbag, as large as a small overnight bag. Snapping the latch behind her she flew out of the room and down the corridor to a back stairway.

Flight after flight she descended, noiseless as a cat. After four or five floors she sped to a fire stairway at the other end of the building. Once, glancing down the hall she thought she saw a man in uniform standing before one of the elevators and she gave the same stifled cry that had escaped her sometimes in the night watches in the seclusion of her own bedcovers.

She hastened on, trying to still the fast beating of her heart and keep her eyes from widening in terror.

One more flight and she'd make it.

She fairly raced down the last stairway, yanked open the fire door and burst out—straight into the arms of a policeman!

Only one horrified gasp she gave and then she was under perfect control. She smiled up into his face, her dimple at its best.

"Oh, I didn't mean to run into you, officer. I'm *so* sorry!" She started to detour but he was too quick for her. He held her wrist in a grasp of iron.

"You're sorry, all right, miss. But we're not. We been waitin' fer you. Come on along."

Gaily Miss Darla swung into step, agreeable, smiling. She chattered as sprightly as a robin and clung so closely to the policeman that it looked for all the world as if they were taking a pleasant walk together. Once her twinkling little feet almost tripped him, she kept so close.

"One more trick like that an' I'll kick ye, miss," quoth the officer. "You ain't so dumb as you look, heh?" He laughed raucously. He led her to a car where two other men, one in uniform and one in plain clothes were waiting.

She smiled charmingly at all of them and bowed as if she were being introduced for the first time. But charm or no charm, they bundled her into the car, and not a word was said until they reached their destination.

Meanwhile Dave was still puzzling over his unexpected ride.

"Can you tell me, sir," he asked his stony-faced companion, "whether this has anything to do with the smashup that I witnessed two weeks ago? I gave my name and offered to tell what I saw, but I have not been called as a witness."

The man scarcely showed that he heard him.

Dave felt helpless, caught in a trap. At last he turned to the only refuge he knew and began to pray silently.

"Lord, I feel as if I'm in the dark again. Help me."

Dave had already formed the habit of slipping his Bible into his pocket when he went out in the morning. Now he thought of it and pulled it out. Detective or no detective, he needed help.

"Lord, I don't know where to turn in this Book. But You have said You won't leave me, and I'm going to trust that You will see me through this jam."

He opened the Book desperately and read whatever his eye fell upon: "The Lord is good, a stronghold in the day of trouble; and He knoweth them that trust in Him."

Dave suddenly laughed aloud.

The other man turned in amazement, glancing down at the Bible and then up at the young man's face with a look of alarm as if he thought he had a maniac in his car. He drove faster.

But Dave continued to stare at the words, his heart growing lighter. He leafed over the pages lovingly as if he would draw strength from them. Then his eye caught another message. "I know the thoughts that I think toward you, saith the Lord, thoughts of peace and not of evil."

Dave could contain himself no longer. He looked at the stony countenance of his captor.

"I—I guess you'll think I'm crazy, sir, but I'm a pretty new Christian, and it's all still wonderful to me. I don't seem to have anybody to turn to but the Lord, and I've found some verses here that sure do make me feel better. Listen." He read them aloud.

"You see, sir, I haven't the slightest idea why you have arrested me, and naturally it isn't a very pleasant feeling. But somehow I know it's going to turn out right. I believe God keeps His promises, don't you?"

The man turned a peculiar look on him and shrugged. But Dave's heart was as light as it had been that first night. What made the difference?

Suddenly they turned a corner and stopped abruptly before an unpretentious building without name or sign of what it was.

Dave was curtly ordered in. Then he was left in an empty room alone for some time. At last his captor returned with another man, evidently a person of some authority.

The two stood gazing at him keenly when all of a sudden a door opposite Dave opened and a girl was led in. It was Darla.

If they had brought the Queen of England Dave could not have been more taken aback.

"Darla!" he exclaimed, surprise, delight and horror mingled in his voice.

Darla smiled back and said in a kittenish tone, "Hi, David," for all the world as if they had met at a picnic unexpectedly.

He looked guilelessly toward the official, bewilderment written all over his countenance.

The officer looked stony.

"Will you please tell us just how long you have known this young lady and how you met her?"

"It was about two weeks ago, sir," said Dave without hesitation, and began eagerly to tell about the accident and how he went with her to the police station.

"I've seen her twice since then, or really three times, but once it was just for a minute or two." He glanced at Darla as if apologizing for mentioning that broken date.

He spoke so frankly and with such obvious pride over his acquaintance with Darla that it was the official's turn to be puzzled.

"Did you ever take Miss Dartman to the plant where you work?"

"No, not yet, sir. We planned to go once, but it fell through. I have promised to take her some other time. I was going to ask permission Monday, sir."

"Are you aware that important secret research is sometimes carried on at the plant?" The man spoke sternly.

"I knew that there must be something like that in the laboratory, sir. I didn't expect to be able to take her through that. In fact I told her I was pretty sure that permission would not be granted for that, only for the helicopter plant."

"She asked to see the laboratory also, did she?"

"Why, y-yes. She is very much interested in science, and airplanes and that sort of thing."

"Yes, she certainly *is!* Young man," he went on looking straight at Dave, "did you know that this girl who calls herself Darla Dartman is a key figure in one of Russia's spy rings?"

Dave started up aghast and sank back, his eyes glued to Darla. Every speck of color drained from his face.

"No! No!" he cried more in agonized protest against the awful statement than in answer to the official's question.

"And," the officer went on mercilessly, "you are known to have visited her more than once in her apartment."

The look on Dave's face at that moment was beyond description.

Dave hadn't been able to take his eyes from Darla's face. He seemed to plead with her to deny the frightful accusation. But as he gazed a horrible change came over her beautiful face. She smiled, but it was a sneering smile, exposing all the evil of her silly little soul. Then she flung at him that slow, mocking laugh.

Dave stared at her in terrible incredulity for a moment and then hid his face in his hands and groaned aloud. The intelligence officers looked at one another significantly over his head.

"Young man, you have been seen at this girl's apartment twice just before important information leaked out."

"Good heavens!" cried Dave in a tortured voice. "I wouldn't know important information if I saw it, and I don't believe Darla would," he added insistently.

"Possibly you don't," rejoined the man coldly. "But she does. And you are just the sort of person she knows how to use. In fact she has made a practice of enticing sentimental young men and officers of the armed forces and using them to get information. You must be aware that this is a serious offence."

"I certainly am, sir," said Dave. His breath came in difficult gasps. "It's the last thing in the world that I would ever want to do. And I—I can't believe Miss Dartman has—has—"

"Believe what you like, young man," came the response brusquely, "but for your own protection we are going to ask you some questions under the lie detector. You may follow us."

Dave's head was in a whirl and his heart felt as if it had suddenly been torn in two. Trembling lest he give a wrong impression by his nervousness, he followed on dumbly, through corridors and up stairways until he was quite confused as to where he was in relation to the street.

They seated him in a room with several other persons and left him. He couldn't tell whether the others were prisoners or officials or guards.

There he waited. Time dragged by. Dave struggled through hour after hour in the dazed agony of disillusionment. All he could think of was Darla. He almost lost sight of his own danger in trying to reconcile what he thought he knew of her with the awful fact of what she must be. He fought the acceptance of it. He kept seeing Darla's face as he had first seen her the day of the accident, shocked and pitiful, like an innocent little lost lamb that needed a strong shepherd.

Oh, it couldn't be true. He vowed that he would never believe it of her unless she admitted it herself. Then her face seemed to come before him wearing that sneering smile and he could hear again her mocking laugh, making light of what they said about her. If she were true and honest, how could she possibly take such an accusation with a laugh? Even he who had done nothing was horrified and shaken at the idea. How much more a lovely innocent girl would feel it, if she *were* lovely and innocent. It was appalling to think that she had deceived him.

Still his heart kept trying to find excuses for her. Surely she didn't realize what a hideous crime she had been guilty of. Hadn't Russia's great spying machine caught her in its ruthless gears to take advantage of her youth and beauty and guilelessness? No, for then she would have been shocked, not amused. Every prop he attempted to use to bolster up her good name only served to prove her treachery.

How had he ever let himself get entangled with such a girl? He stared at the blank wall and rehearsed the events of the past few weeks. What a fool he had been. He remembered how unclean he had felt after that last visit at Darla's! No wonder! The Lord must have been trying to show him that it was no place for him to be. But he had been so set on seeing Darla that nothing else mattered. How blind he had been!

And now she was gone from his life. Would anything ever be the same again? It was like having someone die, someone you had loved with all your might. He began to see now why his father was so bitter. There was nobody to be trusted anywhere. Why not live his own life shut up in his own little sphere? But what would that prove? That was what his father had done. The implication was that everybody else was a hypocrite and he was the only righteous one.

And so he continued to argue with himself. First he was wretched and full of self pity because of losing Darla, then miserable because he had been such a fool as to be deceived by her. He scarcely knew which thought tortured him more.

After eons of misery he heard footsteps coming down the hall and the door opened.

Chapter XVIII

ANNE GAZED anxiously down the hill, glimpsing the road here and there as it wound through the little village. Cars were passing on it constantly, but the few that took their way up the hill went past the stone posts without turning in. Each one was a fresh disappointment. Anne had not realized how much she had looked forward to the little picnic, just she and Dave and her brother together. Of course, she told herself, it was only because she knew Davey enjoyed the young man so much.

The anxiety of not knowing what had befallen Big Dave made her restless, and then, too, there was that little rankling doubt of him. That bothered her worst of all. It seemed disloyal, yet her common sense told her that she really had nothing on which to base a trust in him. As time went on she became more and more aware of how very much she wanted him to ring true.

Davey awoke at last and called her. He was feeling quite frisky until he found that his hero had not returned. That sobered him, but he reassured Anne.

"You know we asked God to take care of him. He's all right, of course."

Anne smiled, but they ate a rather silent lunch. After it was finished she swung the hammock gently for a time, gave Davey a good rub on his legs, and then arose in a businesslike manner and announced that she was going to get to work.

"I'm going to start cleaning 'our' room," she said. Her heart gave a lurch. Perhaps the whole scheme would fall through! What if Dave shouldn't come back? "Oh *God*," she flashed a prayer again, "take care of Dave and let him turn out to be true!" Then she set her pretty chin firmly and went on planning. "I can't do much with the rest of the house without Dave or somebody here to give me the right, but nobody can object if I clean an empty room."

She described the sunny conservatory to Davey and promised that of course they would have some flowers in it that he could take care of himself. She left him happily watching two airplanes high in the sky practicing stunts while she went into the lonely house again.

She swept and dusted and scrubbed steadily for three hours, stepping out occasionally to see that Davey was all right. Then just as she finished the windows and was about to attack the baseboards, she heard the sound of whistling. That must be Dave! Her heart gave a glad leap. If he was whistling everything must be all right.

She hurried out eagerly.

There stood a tall, well-built, gray-haired stranger, talking to Davey. He had a wide, disarming smile and Davey was obviously enjoying him. His car was parked on the driveway, facing the gate, and she could see a little green cross on a tag at its rear bumper. He must be Dave's Dr. Barnhart!

He smiled a welcome. "Of course you are Anne and Davey," he beamed. "Dave has told me about you. I'm sure it is the Lord's doing to bring you here. It's a dreary place, but you'll be able to brighten it up, and the people too," he added. He stood looking down at Anne lovingly, as if he were her own father.

"Where is Dave?" he asked, glancing around.

Anne hesitated. Davey started to speak and looked at her. She nodded.

"I guess there's no harm in telling Dr. Barnhart," she said soberly.

He looked alert. "Something wrong?" he asked.

"Well, we don't know. It's sort of strange." Then she told him what had occurred that morning.

He drew his brows down a moment. "That surely is puzzling." Then he looked up with that wonderful smile again. "I'll look into it. You keep praying. The Lord will work it out. You'll see. I believe the boy is on the level." He looked at his watch. "Nearly two o'clock. I had some calls but they can wait. I'll make inquiries. Do you have a way home?"

Anne shook her head. "No." She gave a laugh. "We're stranded."

He laughed too, as if it were all in the day's fun. "Well, I guess the Lord must have sent me here, for sure. I'll go and see what I can dig up and if Dave doesn't get back I'll come and drive you home. You all right a while, boy? Not too tired?"

Davey shook his head emphatically. "I just love it here, sir," he declared. "And as soon as they let me, I'm going to try to get up. I want to run around and climb all these trees."

The doctor smiled again. "I believe you will, sonny. And not too long hence, either. Good-bye for now. I'll be back soon."

Anne heaved a deep sigh of relief as they watched him take off. He drove swiftly, with purpose, as he did everything, as if he were absolutely sure that what he was doing was the right thing. It was comforting. He was like a bulwark.

Davey was smiling at her.

"*Now* everything will be all right. He's a swell guy."

"Yes," laughed Anne. "He is a swell guy. I hope—"

"There you go again. You don't think God will work things right. But He will. You'll see."

"Oh, Davey, I'm ashamed of myself. Yes, I know He will. Now I'm almost finished in there and then I'll come out and read to you."

It was not long before she came bringing a little stool and sat down beside Davey to read his favorite book about Wilbur and Orville Wright. But her mind was not on the story and her eyes were constantly straying to the road.

Dr. Barnhart went straight to the village police station but it was nearly two hours before he could pull enough wires to find out where Dave was. He caught up with him just as Dave was passing through the hall on his way to the grueling test.

"Poor fellow!" he said to himself. "He looks as if he'd been through the third degree."

Dave saw the doctor before the door closed on him, and it warmed his heart to know that he had a friend nearby. Was it the doctor's smile, or the remembrance of what he stood for that reminded Dave of the messages he had found in his Bible on the way to the city that morning? With an effort he forced himself to recall the words he had read. What a fool he had been not to remember his Bible and look them up again during the hours of waiting. He couldn't bring them all back. His mind was too distraught. But he knew they were something about a stronghold in the day of trouble for those who were trusting the Lord. His heart groped toward God like a wounded soldier toward a foxhole. Instantly his heart was calm. He took his seat and allowed the strange machine to be fastened on him.

When he answered the questions his voice did not tremble nor did he stammer, but it was a long siege. Even Dr. Barnhart was subjected to questioning. Time and again they grew discouraged, but finally, at half-past five, Dave was released with a clean slate. He was fairly bursting with relief and thankfulness when Dr. Barnhart led him to his car and they started home.

"Well, let's have it, son. The whole thing," said the doctor heartily, "It will do you good to talk."

"It's a mess!" replied Dave miserably. There was a deep note of seriousness in his voice and the doctor did not miss it. "But," he added, "the Lord helped me."

"Of course. He's bound to. Go ahead," urged Dr. Barnhart.

"I've been an awful fool," began Dave.

"Of course," agreed the doctor. "We all have in one way or another. Go on."

Dave started with the accident and told everything. He did not try to tone down his own sentimental foolishness. He poured it all out. The doctor listened with keen attention and a deep relief that it was no worse.

When he had told it all Dave said solemnly, "I hope I have learned, Doctor, never to trust a pretty girl again." He was startled to have the doctor throw back his head and roar with laughter.

Dave didn't know whether to be hurt or not. He managed a weak sound like a chuckle. Then the doctor stopped laughing and looked at him.

"Dave," he said, "it's likely that almost every young fellow in the world has said that at one time or another. Son, it's not the pretty face that's the wrong thing. Some of them are good, and some are bad. The trouble was you weren't following your Guide. You know, Dave, God has sent His Spirit to live in your heart. He's a Person. He's there to check you or spur you on. Form the habit of referring everything to Him. He'll let you know what is clean and what is unclean. It's for the sake of His own reputation that He wants to keep you from evil. 'He leadeth me in the paths of righteousness *for His name's sake.'* "

Dave looked at him in awe. "I've heard those words, sir, but I never thought they meant that."

"That's the trouble, Dave, we don't think that God means what He says. We repeat that Twenty-third Psalm over and over and it becomes just a lot of nice words. What else *could* it mean?"

"I don't know, I never thought it meant anything, I guess. That way you put it, it's pretty wonderful. It puts it all up to Him, doesn't it?"

"It does, and He'll never fail. All you have to do is let Him lead you. I should say you have much to be thankful for, Dave."

"I know I have," said Dave humbly.

"I imagine for a while you thought you had had a pretty raw deal from God, didn't you?"

"Well, I don't know as I put it that way, sir. I never thought of God in connection with it for a long time. Then I saw you in the corridor and you reminded me of Him. It had hit me pretty hard. I couldn't believe Darla was false."

"Did you take time to think what your own way would have led you into? You would have liked to go on dating Darla, wouldn't you? Then maybe in the vague future you had thought you might somehow make her love you enough to marry you, didn't you?"

Dave grew very red. "Well, I—I suppose I did think something like that."

"And you were hard hit because you saw you weren't going to get what you thought you wanted? You were tempted to get bitter about it. Suppose God had let you go on? Suppose, for instance, you were married to that girl right now? Do you see what a position you would be in?"

Dave shuddered.

"Now stop pitying yourself," warned the doctor bluntly, "and put your head up and remember that you are a child of God, a member of His family. He has saved you from more than you realize."

"I'm sure He has!" responded Dave penitently. "I'm thoroughly ashamed of myself. It wasn't that the Lord didn't warn me. I even prayed that He would get rid of any sin in my life, but I didn't know that He would really answer. I hadn't even realized this was sin. It seemed as if the prayer just melted away and nothing happened for days, and then this! I see now that I wouldn't have listened if He had done it some easy way."

"Most of us don't, son," sighed the doctor.

"I guess it was like using the scalpel on me, like you said," suggested Dave.

"I guess so," agreed his friend, turning in between the old stone gateposts. "Well, here we are, and speaking of pretty faces, that girl you have picked for your nurse is a winner. She's a jewel."

"Oh? Yes, she's a fine person," said Dave unconcernedly. "But of course she's not the kind you'd fall in love with."

"No? Hm-m," mused the doctor, a twinkle hiding in his gray eyes. "No, of course not."

"No," agreed Dave seriously, climbing out of the car on his side. "Anyway, I'm done with that sort of thing."

The doctor raised his eyebrows in amusement. "Young man," he muttered to himself from the other side of the car, "I'll give you just one month."

Anne had seen them approaching and told Davey, who nearly fell out of the hammock with joy.

Big Dave picked him up and he gave his friend a bear hug that nearly choked Dave and turned his face red.

"You see, Anne, I told you!" Davey flung at his sister.

It was Anne's turn to blush crimson.

Then the doctor interrupted.

"By the way, Dave, I haven't told you yet: your father is a little better. He spoke a few words and was asking for you. You'd better go in tonight if you can."

"Wonderful! Thank you, Doctor, for—everything!"

"Glad I could do it, Dave." They waved farewell to him and turned toward the house.

A slight embarrassed pause crept up on them, until Davey began his chatter about planes. Anne made no reference to what had happened, but at last as they were about to enter the house Dave broke into Davey's conversation.

"I'd better tell you the whole deal, Anne," said Dave humbly. "You might as well know."

Anne noticed his tone and thought to herself,

"He's just as if he had been emptied and scoured and wrung out. It must have been grueling."

"Why don't you wait a little?" she suggested gently. "You need to think about something else for a while. Let's go in and I'll tell you what I have in mind. Davey hasn't seen the house yet, you know."

Somewhat relieved, Dave assented and with Davey on his shoulders riding like a prince, Dave followed Anne inside.

The little boy was enchanted with the big rooms. "So much room to play!" he breathed. But it was Big Dave who was amazed at the sudden change in the old conservatory.

"I don't suppose I've been in here in two or three years," he said. "I can remember when my mother had lots of plants here. She loved them." He spoke wistfully. "You certainly have made it shine. But are you sure you and Davey don't want one of the big bedrooms?"

"I am sure, Dave. You must remember I don't plan to be in it much," she said, making a wry little face. "And I think this is just the place for Davey, with all the sunshine it will get. Think how simple it will be to see to all three patients. They'll be on one floor with the dining room in the center. You and Uncle Harry can stay upstairs," she grinned, "and have a pleasant time together."

Dave guffawed. "Pleasant, my eye! he chortled. I'll stay just as far away from that stinker as I possibly can." Then he stopped short and a cloud came over his face. He suddenly recalled the last time he had used that word. It was in his prayer the other night when he confessed to the Lord that he himself was a stinker. All at once it came to him that if that was so—and it still was, most assuredly—he and Uncle Harry were *both* stinkers in the eyes of the Lord. The only difference was that he had discovered what he was, and Uncle Harry had not.

It then occurred to him to try to tell Uncle Harry. But he realized instantly that that would never do. If someone had tried to tell him, he wouldn't have taken it, not even from a man like Dr. Barnhart. The only way he had had his own eyes opened was through Dr. Barnhart's love and interest.

That created a terrific issue. "Love and interest." Love *Uncle Harry* and show interest in him? Impossible.

While this was running through Dave's mind he had

turned toward the window and was staring out. It was only a second or two between his remark and Anne's answer, but the impression the thought made was painful and deep like the incision of a sharp knife. That must be the scalpel again! Would operations never be over?

Anne told him about her first encounter with Uncle Harry and then she made known her plans and Dave approved them.

"I think I can borrow Mr. Dawson's big truck to move you," he suggested. "That is, if you think it will be safe for your things."

"Oh, that will save a lot," cried Anne joyfully. "I mean," she amended getting a little flustered and turning pink, "of course I'd pay you to do it, but it might be cheaper than movers."

"Now, look here, girl," objected Dave. "If this is to be a family affair, don't let's have any talk of pay. Who knows when *you'll* get any pay? I told you all I can do is buy us food. Unless Aunt Amelia coughs up, pay will be minus."

Anne laughed. "That's the last thing I'm worrying about," she said.

It was time to start back to the city and they put Davey into the back seat.

"I'll be down in two seconds," said Dave. "I'm going to run up and grab a sandwich."

"Oh!" gasped Anne. "You haven't had any lunch? Here, these are two little sandwiches left from ours. We couldn't eat much, to tell you the truth," she confessed with an embarrassed little grin. "You eat these on the way in and after you visit the hospital, you come back and have dinner with us."

"Brother! That sounds good," declared Dave. "I'll take you

right up on that. There's scarcely any grub in the house. That is, I suppose Uncle Harry has a shelf full, but I never go in there." At the thought of the old man he frowned again. The issue kept turning up, like Banquo's ghost. He'd have to do something about it. He wasn't going to take a chance again of not heeding the Lord's direction.

Dave left them at Pearl Street and drove to the hospital. His father was improved enough to be able to talk a little, not plainly, but they could carry on a desultory conversation. Dave told him he had arranged for somebody to stay at the house all the time.

"She's not exactly a practical nurse," he explained, trying to stick strictly to the truth, "but she's had a good deal of experience, and Dr. Barnhart approves of her." He added that recommendation on the spur of the moment. He had been apprehensive of his father's reaction to having a woman around the place. He had decided to tell him as little as possible and then let him find out the rest when it happened. He said nothing about Davey. After all, if he was taking care of the expenses himself, he surely had the right to select his employee.

So, without knowing it, he left his father with the vague impression of a solid, middle-aged woman who would do the chores and run his errands.

Then Dave stopped on the next floor to see Aunt Amelia. He was aware that she was quite a different proposition.

As he walked into the room the first thing he saw was the evening paper spread out at the foot of her bed and in the middle of the front page under glaring headlines was Darla's picture!

Chapter XIX

Just the sight of her beautiful face brought all his wretchedness back upon him. The headline read:

BEAUTY CONVICTED OF
STEALING SECRETS

Dave stared at the face of the girl he had thought he loved. If only she had been what she had seemed to be. But all he could see now was the sneer in her smile. What a deliverance!

He wanted to snatch the paper and read. Was his own name blazoned there? If it was, Aunt Amelia would certainly see it and make the most of it. He wrenched his eyes from the picture and steadied himself. His aunt was far enough now on the road to recovery to be her old fault-finding self. It would not be an easy interview, in any case.

"How are you, Aunt Amelia?" he asked in what he hoped was a genial tone.

"Oh-h!" she groaned. "I'm in terrible shape. It's you, is it? It's about time you came to see your poor old aunt, after all these weeks."

"Why, Aunt Amelia, I've been in four or five times to see you," reminded Dave.

"Four or five times! Don't try to hand me that, you young scamp. I guess I know who has been in and who has deliberately stayed away." She always spoke in a hoarse, deep voice, "sort of rattley," Dave used to call it when he was a boy, "like a snare drum."

198

"You're just like your hardhearted father," she went on. "He wouldn't come near his own sister that has looked out for him all these years, not if I was dying."

"Aunt Amelia," Dave began patiently.

"Oh, don't 'Aunt Amelia' me, trying to stand up for *him*. I know how he feels about me."

"Dad is here, in the hospital," stated Dave bluntly.

"He is?" Amelia snatched at his words. "Well, why doesn't he come up, then. *I* know. He hates me. The only sister he's got. I made your Uncle Harry take him in when he was homeless, but he hates me for it."

Ordinarily Dave would have blazed out that his father had just as much right in the house as she, and more than Uncle Harry, but this time he only said,

"Dad's had another stroke. It was the worst of all."

Aunt Amelia was actually silent for a few moments. Then, "Humph!" she snorted. "I'm not surprised. Well, he can't expect *me* to nurse him this time. And I can't hire him anybody. I'm done helping him, I tell you. I'm spending every cent I had laid up on this hospital business. And what I'm going to do when I'm out of here, I don't know. Your uncle can't nurse me, and it's certain your father can't, and wouldn't if he could. Oh-h," groaned the poor old woman, "it's pitiful when a good woman spends her life looking after other people and then is left friendless and penniless at the end when she needs help herself." Aunt Amelia managed to make it sound as if she were shedding tears, although Dave doubted their existence. He had long ago decided that Aunt Amelia's cold heart had congealed all the tear glands in her big selfish body. But he still spoke patiently.

"I have arranged for a nurse, Aunt Amelia," he said as gently as he was able. "She will be living in the house and has agreed to take care of both you and Dad."

"You have hired a nurse," Amelia roared. "And who is to pay her, I'd like to know? You, with your boy-earnings? Or your pauper father? A nurse! Do you know how much it costs to have a nurse, child?"

Wickedly Dave saw his opportunity. In a guileless voice he said, "Why no, Aunt Amelia, I haven't asked. How much?"

She sputtered with indignation and tried to raise herself up to have a better vantage to fling her fury at him.

"*I* have inquired here at the hospital. They tell me it would be impossible to get even a practical nurse, part time, for a cent less than forty dollars a week. It's outrageous. And who could pay that?"

Dave smiled. He had his advantage. She had committed herself.

"But if I tell you that I have one full time, and you need pay only half, that isn't so outrageous. At any rate, it's got to be."

"Got to be?" she almost screamed. "Who says it's got to be? Don't think you can begin to order me around, you young rascal."

"I have no desire to order you around, Aunt Amelia," answered Dave quietly. "You can take it or leave it. You said yourself you can't get anybody for less than forty. If you don't want this girl for twenty, then we'll take her part time and you can get some other person for forty."

Aunt Amelia was too smart not to know that she was caught. She stormed and spluttered but Dave was unmoved.

"How much do you earn, that you can afford twenty dollars a week?" she demanded once.

Dave did some quick thinking. It wouldn't do to tell her that, it was none of her business.

"I'll be glad to tell you," he replied in a too gentle

tone, "when you tell me how much you have salted away, in bonds."

She exploded at that and called him an insolent brat.

He let her rave and calmly reached over and picked up the paper and began to read it. "If she has seen my name here she'll be sure to start in on that," he thought to himself. "But I'll tell her absolutely nothing." He glanced hastily through the writeup.

"Pretty American-born blonde turns traitor to her country and uses her beauty and brains to pry secrets from American officers and research workers. The court is shielding the identity of several intelligence officers high in official circles who have been duped by her wiles. Her activities have been far-reaching however, since she is able to speak five languages fluently. In the past weeks there have been several leaks in important information calculated to be useful to an enemy. These have led to the arrest of this girl and a few others whose names are withheld at present."

That was all. Dave heaved a deep sigh of relief. The Lord was good to him. He felt as if he was willing to take all of Aunt Amelia's raging and more, in gratitude for his wonderful deliverance.

He had been only dimly aware of her railing and her dramatic silences while he was reading. Now he came back to her presence as it were, from that dreary room at the FBI headquarters to which the newspaper account had carried him.

She was saying that if she was going to have to pay something for a nurse she felt it was her right to see the woman first and decide whether or not she wanted her.

Dave put his foot down.

"Aunt Amelia," he stated in a determined tone, rising and

standing above her, "I've hired this girl and she is the one I'm going to have. Not only that, but I've told her she can do as she likes about rearranging things in the house to make it convenient for her. If you don't like the plans I've made or you don't like her, you can see to getting your own help. I'm offering to let you in on it. You will not do better. I know that, and you know it. You can think it over. Good night." And Dave walked out leaving her to storm all by herself.

"She'll come around all right," he chuckled to himself. "What else can she do? And I've got her pinned down to paying Anne twenty dollars a week. It's not much, for the job she will have to do, but it's something."

He had a gay time recounting to Anne his interview with his aunt. She was just a little horrified at first at Dave's forthright management of the salary question, but he was firm.

"It's little enough," he insisted. "And I *know* she has plenty. You are not to give in to her a little bit, nor take the money apologetically. If I could have wangled twice that out of her I'd have done it."

Davey beamed with glee, not understanding very clearly what it was all about, but he knew that Big Dave was effecting some deal to the advantage of Anne. He had utmost faith in Big Dave.

After the supper was cleared away, Anne discovered that she was out of milk for Davey the next day.

"I can run down to that corner drugstore and get some. It will still be open," she said.

"I'll go for you," offered Dave. "Or better still, I'll take you. Then you can get what else you may want. Will Davey mind?"

"No, he's used to being alone. I'll tuck him up for the night. He's had a big day and he ought to get to sleep."

Davey assented happily and they went out.

Dave started to get the car, but Anne said, "Why not walk? It's such a little way."

"Fine," agreed Dave. They swung off together, Anne trying to stretch her steps to match his long ones. He helped her courteously up and down curbs. It felt good to have a big escort beside her who took care that she didn't stumble in the darkness. She stole a glance up at him once or twice. He certainly was a man in a thousand, for looks at least.

Dave's eyes were straight ahead. Aside from the automatic courtesies he performed, Anne might have been a wooden statue for all the notice he took of her. The story of his foolishness weighed heavily on his mind. He could not feel at ease until Anne knew it. There was no peace in having something to hide all the time.

After they bought the milk he said,

"Let's walk around by the park. I want to tell you what happened today."

They passed through the noisy streets, a tense silence upon them both. The commotion of the city dwellers moving hither and thither was a businesslike restlessness, unlike the turmoil in Dave's mind. That was depressing. Anne's heart went out to him. What miserable revelation would he make? He had seemed so fine and true, she dreaded to discover anything that would destroy the ideal of him that her heart had built up. Yet there was sin in everybody. Why should she think there should be none in him?

They took a seat on a bench in a secluded section of the grassy square. For the first time he seemed to be aware of her. He turned his face toward her in the moonlight and opened his mouth to speak. Then dropped his head and turned away. Her heart ached for him.

"Don't tell, if you'd rather not," she said gently.

"No, I want to." He forced the words in a strained voice. "It's not a pretty story, but I want you to know. If we're to be working together, I don't want to have a skeleton that might turn up some time."

Anne waited. He was glad of her silence. Some girls would have chattered to cover the embarrassment of the moment.

At last he began. He spoke in a low tone, in short jerky sentences, as if he could force only a few words at a time.

"You remember the day of the accident?"

Anne nodded. He could see her earnest face turned up to his in the moonlight. How he hated to bring a look of scorn and distrust there. She appeared to have such confidence in him. She wouldn't soon, not after he told her. She would shrink away in disgust.

"Well, I tried to help that other girl," he went on. "I saw there were plenty of people looking after you, and she just sat there stunned. At least I thought she was frightened and didn't know what to do. She was shaking all over. I even had to find her license for her. Then I went to the police station with her. I knew the smashup was all her fault, and that was the reason I thought she needed help. I—I fell pretty hard for her, I guess. I had never seen anyone like her." He stopped and glanced at Anne. She simply waited. Only the tense clasping of her hands showed she was feeling deeply with him.

"I promised her I would hunt you up and report to her how you were. I see now that that was all my own idea. She didn't ask me to, and when I did report to her, she didn't care. I don't know why I didn't recognize that right away. I was a fool. She must have had many a laugh at me. I thought of course she would be concerned for you, because she knew it was her fault that you were hurt. It was a long time before I realized that her only concern was what might happen to her. She is absolutely selfish, through and through."

Anne drew a soundless little breath that Dave didn't hear. He spoke rapidly now, anxious to have it over with.

"I only came to see you on her account, and I was afraid you would see that and resent it. When the nurse got your brother and me confused, I was relieved to be able to do something for you to prove—to myself, I guess, that I was sincerely trying to help. Then when I met Davey, he was such a game little kid and seemed to take to me, I couldn't disappoint him. As I think it all over now, I can see God's hand in it. It must have been his plan that I meet you two. It's funny but I'm beginning to be almost glad it all happened. When I think how I would have gone on in the old way, in darkness, I see how wonderful it was that God took the trouble to get me in a jam."

Anne's eyes were alight with a radiance that outshone the moonlight but Dave didn't see it. He was staring straight ahead now, trying to get up the courage to tell the rest.

"After I met that girl"—he found it difficult even to mention her name to Anne, there seemed to be such a vast distance between the two—"I guess I didn't have my mind on anything else. I had never bothered with girls before, and I couldn't believe that such a gorgeous person as she was would look at me. I never did tell her much about myself. She asked my address but she never came out. I'm glad. She would not have understood like you do. I've never told anybody about the mess at home."

Gently Anne laid her hand on his knee a moment, just to let him know that she appreciated his confidence.

"She lived in a swank apartment and she invited me up a

couple of times. It looked good to me to have a friend; at least I thought she'd be a friend. But now I know she was just taking me for a ride. I never would have believed a person could seem so sweet and be so rotten. It took something like what happened this morning to shake me out of my silly dream.

"She found out where I worked and asked me to take her to see the plant. She pretended to be interested in helicopters. I tried to get permission to go through. I should have known then that there was something wrong going on. The office took her name and address and held me up a long time. We never did get the pass. This morning that was an FBI officer who took me in for questioning. They had her there at headquarters. It seems she had been making a business of getting information about army plans, through officers and anybody she could get into her net. I was one of the little flies that walked into her parlor."

Dave's head was down and it seemed to Anne that all the bitterness of his life must be wrung out of him as he confessed his shame and foolishness.

"I still didn't want to believe what she was, and it wasn't until she looked at me and laughed, a horrible laugh full of mockery, that I realized it was all true. It hit me hard, harder than I like to admit. But," he raised his head and spoke with relief, in a clear voice, "I'm *glad* it happened. That's about all. I wanted you to know."

He turned and looked full into Anne's face as if daring her to trust him now. She looked steadily back at him.

"If you want to cancel our agreement, you can," he offered. "I wouldn't blame you."

"Why should that affect my coming out there to nurse your father?" asked Anne quietly.

"Because you might not want to be mixed up in it. My name's down there in the records of the FBI now. You have only my word for it that I'm not in the spying business too."

"They didn't keep you there, I notice," smiled Anne.

"No. But how do you know I'm telling you the whole truth?"

"You didn't have to tell me any of it, did you?"

"No," he answered sadly. "It wasn't fun, either. It could make you disgusted with me."

"It doesn't," she said simply.

He turned again and looked into her face. She returned his frank gaze and they smiled, a slow, warm, understanding smile. Something that had been uncomfortable and restless inside Dave all his life seemed to settle down in peace. He drew a deep breath.

"I believe," he said solemnly, "that you are what I'd call a real friend. I've never had one before, at least not until I met Dr. Barnhart. A friend, I think, is somebody who knows the worst about you and doesn't throw you over for it."

"Who am I to throw you over?" said Anne, a queer little touch of sadness in her tone. "Don't you think I've done my share of foolish things?"

"No. I can't imagine you being anything but what you ought to be," he said seriously.

She laughed ruefully. He thought there were tears behind her voice when she spoke, measuring her words. "I fell for somebody once, too," she confessed, "when I was in college. He was a lot older than I and worthless, I guess. It was only the Lord who opened my eyes in time to keep me from a lot of trouble. We're all a foolish lot of sinners, Dave. The Lord is good to us."

"You said it!" he exclaimed fervently.

He tucked Anne's hand under his arm and quite naturally they walked arm in arm enjoying a sweet companionable understanding.

"I can't get over the Lord's goodness in stopping me before it was too late," Dave kept saying. "It makes me wonder whether there aren't other things in my life that He may disapprove of. I think I'll have a thorough house-cleaning tonight, on my knees."

They were at the Pearl Street house and Anne paused before she opened the door to go in.

Once more she looked up at him, searching his face and reveling in his sincerity. She scarcely trusted herself to speak.

"I guess it's a good thing for all of us, every so often," she said softly.

Dave reached for her hands and held them firmly, warmly, a moment. He looked earnestly into her upturned face.

"You don't know what it means to me," he said tenderly, "that you still believe in me."

"Why shouldn't I?" she responded softly.

"Plenty of reasons. You're—terrific!" he breathed as he let her go and strode off to his car. And he never knew that he was saying the very words that Darla had used to him.

He sang as he drove home. How good it was to get things straightened out with God and with all the people concerned. Now, he determined, he was going to meet that "love Uncle Harry," issue and win. "With God you can't lose," the doctor had said.

He parked under the silent porte-cochere and entered the dark hall. Then he stopped short. Somebody was fumbling with the door knob at the end of the hallway.

CHAPTER XX

HE SWITCHED on the light as the door opened and came face to face with Uncle Harry.

Dave blinked. In the change from darkness to the bright light of the hall, he could not discern the man's features plainly, to tell whether he came in war or peace.

But Dave found himself taking the initiative.

"Oh, hello, Uncle Harry," he greeted him, "I was going to hunt you up. Thought maybe you'd like to drive in to the hospital with me tomorrow. I'll be ready about two. I'm going down to church in the village in the morning." Dave didn't care particularly whether his uncle accepted or not. But he felt that he had made the first step which was required of him. If this was an answer to his prayer, it was rather breathtaking to find the answer ready almost before he had asked.

Uncle Harry made a noise in his throat, whether of amazement or appreciation, it was impossible to distinguish.

"Hjerrup!" He always had to clear his throat before he spoke, like a player warming up before going into a game. "A' right," he replied laconically. Then he vouchsafed a few more words, evidently the ones he had planned to say when he came in. "I got somethin' I want to talk to you about."

"Okay," responded Dave as pleasantly as he could. "See you tomorrow," he added through the closed door, for Uncle Harry had turned and left him unceremoniously.

Now what? From his uncle's tone of voice the talk was not anything to look forward to. Dave felt as if he had done all that could be expected of him. Or had he? He felt around in his heart for the peace he had hoped for. There was still a measure of unrest. He sought for the approval of the Lord, but he wasn't sure whether he had obeyed fully the strange prompting. Puzzled, he trudged upstairs.

The next afternoon Uncle Harry was on hand and already seated in the car when Dave came down.

As usual, Uncle Harry was slow in getting at his conversation. At last, after Dave had made some remarks on the weather and Aunt Amelia's condition, without any response at all from the other man, Uncle Harry suddenly said,

"This girl you've hired for a nurse—" Dave took a deep breath prepared to stand his ground, "you're planning to pay her, are you?"

"I've already talked that over with Aunt Amelia," replied Dave trying to hold his patience.

"Well, she says you want her to pay, and I'm not going to let my wife be milked. We've talked it over, too. We think she's done enough fer you and yer pop. It seems little enough you could do to see that yer aunt's taken care of when she's helpless." Uncle Harry spoke with heat.

In a desperate attempt to keep out of a quarrel, Dave held his tongue, trying to think what to answer. His uncle took his silence for insolence.

"Well?" he demanded.

Dave still waited, so he went on snarling:

"You needn't think, you half-baked pup, that you and yer pop can do us out of what little we have left."

"Uncle Harry," Dave began, using all his self-control, "I am not aware that you or Aunt Amelia have done anything at all for me and Dad except to help make the house a place of misery. You know perfectly well that the property was awarded by the court to both Aunt Amelia and my father equally, in the absence of a will. Please let's not go into that again."

"That may be. But," persisted the man, "who has taken the heavy end of the expenses all this time? And what has yer pop ever done to keep up the value of the place?"

"And you?" Dave retorted, biting his lips to keep from calling names.

"I'm a sick man," whined Harry. "There were plenty of years when yer pop could have worked but he was too proud."

Dave ground his teeth. The same old complaints, the same old retorts, each side trying to vindicate itself.

"Oh, Lord!" he appealed. "What do I do now?"

He half expected some miracle, at least as astonishing as the way Uncle Harry had turned up in the house last night. But the only word that came to his mind was "stinker." He all but burst out with it. It was Dave's favorite word to express contempt to the uttermost. "Stinker! Stinker!" How he would love to use it now. That's exactly what Uncle Harry was, a stinker.

But the very recollection of the word drove him to think of that other recent time he had used it, when he had been talking to the Lord about himself. He and Uncle Harry were *both* stinkers! Then, who was he to criticize his uncle? That was the very thing that a man at the plant had done the other day, complained of a fellow worker to the boss. Every man in the place despised him for it, even the boss himself.

"Lord!" exclaimed Dave in his heart. "Am I like that in your eyes?" And suddenly the whole matter took on a different light. It was bad enough for both him and his uncle to *be* stinkers, but he had gone whining to God with complaint about the other man! What a worm he was.

But Uncle Harry was feeling anything but wormy. Failing to catch the swift acid retort that any mention of his father's faults always brought from Dave, he decided that his own remark must have missed fire somehow, and he tried again.

"Ain't noticed *you* ever doin' anything to hurt yourself around the place, either," he prodded. "Fur as I can see, you're jest a dad-blum lazy good-fer-nothin' like him."

This sort of talk had never failed to keep the battle going briskly. But this time, after a moment of deep silence, Dave replied contritely,

"I guess you're about right, Uncle Harry. I've begun to see that I have never been much account. I'm ashamed of myself."

It was the first statement that Dave had ever made to his uncle with absolute sincerity, without any attempt to make some impression, good or bad. It took Harry Mathers completely off balance. And as for Dave, he was just as much surprised. Instead of feeling like a worm, he had a swift sense of gladness and warmth, like being in a secure haven with nothing to worry about. Why, he hadn't felt like this since the night he had taken Christ as his Saviour. This was the strangest thing of all the strange things that had happened since that night. He suddenly felt like singing again. He almost forgot poor Uncle Harry sitting there beside him, weaponless, his darts all turned aside.

The man stole a sidelong glance at his nephew. Never in all his fifty-odd years had he ever heard him or anyone else abuse himself like that. What further attack could he make? He was flabbergasted.

As no more was said, Dave was left free to revel in his newly recovered joy. He started to whistle.

Having gone so far, Dave spoke to his uncle in a friendly, carefree voice.

"You know, Uncle Harry, last week I took Jesus Christ as my Saviour and it's made a tremendous difference. I had no business speaking as I did when we started out. I must confess, I have had some pretty bitter thoughts about you. I hope you will forgive me. When I think of how much the Lord has forgiven me, I don't see any sense in my finding fault with somebody else."

Uncle Harry did not answer, but all at once Dave's joy could not be contained and he burst out with the words of the song he had been whistling:

"I hold not the Rock, but the Rock holds me . . ."

For five more miles Uncle Harry didn't open his mouth. Dave grinned to himself. It was not only marvelous, but *fun* to see how the Lord could work when you really let Him do it His way.

But he soon realized that he hadn't yet learned all the various kinds of tests that a child of God could be put through. Uncle Harry began again: "Hjerrup!"

"Here it comes," thought Dave. "What'll it be now?" From the very tone of his voice in clearing his throat, Dave could tell that something of an evil nature had been seething inside his uncle and now it was about to come to a boil.

"You good-fer-nothing impudent pup!" he exploded, adding a choice string of less desirable names, "if you think you can get anywheres with me on that religious line, you can shut yer cursed mouth. I'm fed up with ya." He craned his scrawny neck around until his discolored eyes peered sidewise into Dave's. "I'm warnin' you. *This* is the *end.* Yer aunt an' me have talked this thing over plenty. You gotta git out. We

ain't gointa put up with you. I'll give ya five days, countin'
today, *an' no more!*"

His smelly pipe went back between his yellow crooked
teeth and he chewed it mercilessly. He was breathing fast. It
had taken a great deal out of him to take that stand, but he
felt that the rights of the Mathers had been upheld.

At first Dave wanted to laugh. Then the old favorite word
"stinker" crept to the tip of his tongue. *"Little* stinker"
would be appropriate and would hurt more, used with a
mocking laugh. But the very word reminded him of what he
had but just said to his uncle. And who had used a mocking
laugh like a sword but the girl whose evil nature had got
him into trouble? Human anger and human words were not
weapons for a child of God to use.

Again Dave was surprised to hear his own voice saying:
"I'm sorry you feel that way about me, Uncle Harry. If it
were possible just now for me to leave I would be more than
glad to do so. But I have a responsibility to my father, if not
to your wife who is my aunt, and I guess I'll have to stay and
carry it out. Dad will be home Sunday and I've got to see
that he is taken care of."

Only a snort of anger and a muttered curse were Uncle
Harry's reply. Dave was unruffled by the conversation and
rejoiced that he had been kept from saying any of the hateful
things that had risen to his mind. As for his uncle's order
about leaving the house, he took it lightly as a mere threat
and forgot it.

Dave was so radiant when he went into his aunt's room
she stopped in the middle of a complaint and stared at him.

"How are you, Aunt Amelia?" he greeted her gaily, without any sign of the tension and forced friendliness that had

always been very obvious whenever he spoke to either of his relatives.

But she snapped at him.

"How well do you think I could be? Strung up like a fiddle and not a soul to get me even a drink of water," she moaned in her coarse husky voice. "I declare! If I ever get out of this bed, I'm going to report some of these nurses to the authorities."

Dave winced. How ugly her complaint sounded. Did he sound that way to the ear of God?

He got her the water and tried to say something kind and comforting but unfortunately her bad eyelid fell like a wink just at the wrong moment. It had never failed to affect Dave with inward laughter. He dared not speak. And besides that, each time he opened his mouth Aunt Amelia interrupted with her complaining.

At last he gave it up, saying aloud whether she heard it or not, "I'm going to run up and see Dad. I'll be back for you, Uncle Harry."

The man gave no answer, but Dave was used to that. He would stop for him anyway. He made arrangements at the desk in the corridor to take his father home on Sunday, and then went in and visited a little while with him. He was discouraged that his father seemed to make so little improvement. But the doctor had warned him in the beginning that each stroke was bound to be worse than the last, and that after each one the patient would never quite regain his former health.

There was very little he could use for conversation with his father. Most subjects were taboo because they might excite him or cause worry. The weather, or some little anecdote of the day's work were about all. But this time Dave had brought his Bible and after a few minutes he drew it out and turned to the Twenty-third Psalm.

"I'm going to read to you a little, Dad," he began. "Something that has meant a lot to me lately.

" 'The Lord is my Shepherd, I shall not want. He maketh me to lie down in green pastures. He leadeth me beside the still waters. He restoreth my soul. He leadeth me in the paths of righteousness for His name's sake.' "

Dave lingered tenderly over those words. He read slowly, as if he were sharing something very precious with his father. Then when he finished the Psalm he turned to the Gospel of John and read, "For God so loved the world that He gave His only begotten Son that whosoever believeth in Him should not perish, but have everlasting life."

"Dad," he went on very quietly, "I've just lately learned to trust Him as my Saviour and He's wonderful. I hope you will, too."

That was all. Then he did something he had never done in his life since he was a tiny boy. He leaned over and touched his lips to his father's forehead.

" 'Night, Dad," he said gently, and slipped out.

He didn't know whether his father had heard. He gave no sign. But it had seemed the natural thing to do, to read, and to show that little sign of his love. How strange to find that he did love his father. If he had been asked a few weeks ago whether he loved him or not he would have had to shrug and say, he didn't know, probably not. It seemed that there was nothing that God could not accomplish.

When Dave went back to Aunt Amelia's room Uncle Harry had already gone home. The Dawsons had been in, and finding Uncle Harry there they had offered to give him a ride home. Dave was actually disappointed.

He went out to his car with the intention of going right home but for some reason he found himself headed toward Pearl Street. Strange how eagerly he looked forward to visiting in that tiny home at the back of the dingy hall!

The soft sound of murmuring voices ceased suddenly when he knocked. He waited. There was no opened door, no eager welcome. He had not realized how much he counted on it.

Puzzled, he knocked again.

"Who is it?" Anne called peremptorily, with a note of fear in her voice.

"Big Dave," he answered in his big cheery bass. "I won't keep you a minute."

"Oh!" she cried in relief and joy, and rushed to unlock the door.

Both Anne and Davey seemed distraught and he looked anxiously from one to the other.

"Have I barged in at the wrong time?" he asked hesitatingly.

"No," they both answered in chorus. "No *indeed*," repeated Anne. "I'm glad you are here." She sounded a bit breathless. Dave glanced at her with concern. His look brought the pink to her cheeks and he couldn't help thinking how like a wind-tossed flower she looked.

"Tell him, Anne," begged Davey. Then impulsively he tossed his head. "*I* will. That reporter man was here, the newspaper man, you know, that lives on this floor. He tried to get in. He was *drunk!*" Davey ended in a loud whisper.

Anne was flustered, and tried to pass off the incident but Dave was troubled.

"That settles it," he said soberly. "I'm glad I turned up. It's not good for you two to be here alone. You're coming out tomorrow, to *stay*. I'll bring you in to school the rest of the week, Anne, and I'll get Mrs. Dawson to run over and see to Davey occasionally during the day.

"Boy, oh *boy*," Davey crowed. "Tomorrow!"

Anne smiled and thought a moment. "I suppose it would be sensible," she said slowly.

Dave grinned. "Good! I guess I don't need to talk you into it."

Anne suddenly crimsoned. "I'm as eager as Davey, I guess," she admitted shyly.

They had a gay time, and before Dave left they had planned their departure for the morrow.

But when Dave went back to the old dreary house that night he thought it had never seemed so lonely. He could scarcely wait for tomorrow. As he fell asleep he kept seeing Anne moving about in the big rooms, filling them with her ready laughter, her gentle touches here and there. He must be careful not to let her work too hard. He would try to be on hand as much as possible to help her. Why did the thought of it seem so delightful?

Chapter XXI

Until her furniture should come for the conservatory, Anne selected a temporary room for herself and Davey over the kitchen in what had been the servants' quarters.

"That's what I am, you know," she reminded Dave severely, while she tied on a ruffled pink apron that made her look anything but severe. "This is a regular job, even though there may be some pleasant things about it." She threw him just the wraith of a look that left him wondering just what she referred to as the pleasant things.

"Okay," he agreed. "Just as you say. Most servants nowadays do order their masters around!" He grinned across the pile of Anne's blankets he was carrying.

Something in his smile brought an extra sparkle to Anne's eyes and her ready laugh rang out like merry bells.

They worked swiftly, stopping only to eat the cold supper Anne had prepared that morning. She tucked Davey into bed and then said,

"Good-bye now. I'm going down to beard Uncle Harry in the kitchen. I take it you won't want to come?"

"Sure I'll come," laughed Dave. "Uncle Harry and I are buddies now, even though he did blow his stack, and order me to leave." He told her about their trip in to town.

"Let me go alone first," she insisted, "and make him understand that I'm going to barge into his domain and take over. I've got to clean that place before I'm willing to get a meal there."

She went bravely down the back stairs and knocked at the kitchen door.

She heard a surprised "Hjerrup!" Then, "C'min."

There he was, pipe in hand, seated with his knees crossed beside the old oilcloth-covered table. Anne wondered how long that cover had been on that table.

She gave him a winning smile. This time she knew better than to startle him by offering her hand.

"How are you this evening, Mr. Mathers?"

"Huh!" he grumped.

"My little brother and I have come out a day or two early, to get acquainted with where things are so that I'll be able to do a better job of taking care of our patients when they come. I don't suppose you will mind my coming in here to work a little, will you? You must tell me what you like to eat, you know," she smiled charmingly, "so that I can keep the whole family happy. I do love to cook. Do you like lemon meringue pie, sir?"

She rattled on as she took stock of the place and made silent decisions. He was always so far behind her in his slow thinking that he never answered her swift questions, so they turned out to be merely rhetorical, for the sake of dramatic effect.

By the time he got around to realizing what she was there for, she had stacked up the dirty dishes, discovered the cleaning powder and some rags, and set about scrubbing up the stove and sink. She had made up her mind that that sink had to be scoured before she would even be willing to wash the dishes.

"It's kind of hard for a man, I think," she said sympathetically, "to try to keep up with cooking and cleaning and washing, along with all his other work."

Anne preferred to keep up the pretense that he had any "other work." She determined that before long he would have some, if it was only peeling potatoes.

All at once she stepped to the back stairs with swift determination and called cheerily,

"Dave, oh Dave! Could you come down and help a few minutes?"

The melodious sound of a woman's voice startled the very cobwebs in the corners. Such a sound had not been heard there since the pretty Mrs. Truscott left twelve years ago. And even her voice had not had the merry trilling note that Anne's had, as if she had birds hidden somewhere about her.

Dave had been hovering not far from the top of the stairs, somewhat taken aback that Anne had gone off without him. They had worked and planned together so much that he had begun to count on her wanting him. What a pal she was!

Her call pleased him. Perhaps she missed him a little.

"Coming," he called, and ran down eagerly.

As if he had a right to be there, Anne accepted his entrance into the kitchen that he had scarcely darkened for years. She kept up a constant chatter of gay remarks and directions.

She set him to cleaning the dining room.

"Because," she explained, "we'll all be eating in there now, since I can't be upstairs and down both at the same time. It's such a cozy, comfortable room, too."

Then, while she scrubbed the old oilcloth till it fairly came apart from shock, she continued,

"We'll have to get a new suit for this table, won't we, Mr. Mathers?" She included him in her merry laughter. "I just know you're going to wish I wouldn't disturb you and all these things you have been accustomed to for years, but I'll try to make up for your inconvenience. By the way, I'll bet you didn't cook yourself much dinner tonight. I know how a man is when he's alone. Why don't I slide some cookies in the oven? And we'll make a nice cool drink. It's so warm tonight. I have a box of cookie mix I brought with me. I won't always give you cans and mixes," she laughed, "but you'll have to take what there is until I get going."

She flew up the back stairs again and came down with her box and in a surprisingly few minutes the delicious odor of fresh baking floated in to Dave in the dining room.

He came to the door.

"Don't tell me it's food!" he cried delightedly. "Already?" He was about to tease Anne by telling her that her salary was doubled but he remembered and stopped himself just in time. That would be the worst possible remark to make in front of Uncle Harry.

But he caught a glint of a twinkle in her eyes and realized that she understood.

She always seemed to understand without words. It was as if they were in a covenant together to make this thing a success. It was a warm, comfortable thought. Was there another person in the world whom the Lord could have selected to fill this particular need? Uncle Harry didn't seem to be melting, but anyone except Uncle Harry would, thought Dave, watching Anne's capable little hands. They were dainty hands, yet they seemed to know how to do common tasks well.

While they all sampled the baking, she perched on the edge of the table swinging her feet, and Dave leaned against the wall, his glass in one hand and two or three cookies in the other. He didn't feel free to sit down in Uncle Harry's kitchen.

"Brother!" he exclaimed, "this is worth working for. I'll clean any time if you'll feed me like this." He had a pleasant sense that Anne knew that he would be glad to clean or do anything else that was needed, without cookies or cold drink. She understood that he was just making cheery conversation.

Uncle Harry relaxed his hold on his pipe long enough to munch a few sweetmeats, though he said nothing about them either good or bad. It was impossible to tell what his impassive silence indicated.

Anne and Dave worked another hour or so, and finally she called it enough for the night. She had laid out some of her own dainty place mats at four places around the big round dining room table, set a pretty red bowl filled with gnerly apples from Uncle Harry's storeroom in the center and laid silver and dishes enough for breakfast.

Dave stood and stared at it in wonder. What a change already! It looked like a home!

Uncle Harry was still seated in his chair beside the kitchen table. He had not stirred all the evening. But Dave was glowing.

"You mean we're to have a real breakfast, *here,* right away tomorrow morning?"

"You guessed correctly, Mr. Truscott," said Anne, sparkling her pleasure that he was pleased.

"Will wonders never cease?" he exclaimed. "Say," he lowered his voice and came over near her, "you sort of have the old bird eating out of your hand, haven't you?"

"Don't shout too soon. He hasn't committed himself," whispered Anne, starting up the stairs. "And besides, the female is still deadlier than the male. Food may work wonders with him, but there is no infallible road to his wife's heart. We shall have to tread softly and pray. If we conquer that citadel it will be only by the grace of God." Anne spoke very seriously.

"That's for sure," agreed Dave.

Anne found Davey sleeping soundly and she crawled in with him thankfully, for she was very weary. She sincerely hoped that all of her work would not have to be done under the deadly pall of that man's presence.

The first breakfast together was a joy. Anne had risen early and fixed orange juice, delicate scrambled eggs, and toast. The food was from Dave's supplies, but she had raided Aunt Amelia's pantry and discovered some of her home-made jelly.

She knocked on Uncle Harry's door when it was almost time to sit down, but there was no answer. She knocked again and called cheerily that breakfast was ready. Still no response. She and Dave had to go to work, so they decided to proceed without him.

"I'll be surprised if you can get him to eat with us," said Dave shaking his head doubtfully. "That's a big concession. It practically makes him admit that we're fit to live with."

"Well, he's going to do it or get his own," stated Anne with quiet determination. There was a flash to her pretty brown eyes and a set to her chin that made Dave smile.

They had brought Davey down and, eyes alight, he asked permission again to give thanks for the food.

"Oh dear, dear Lord Jesus," he said earnestly, "thank You so much for this nice place, and for the food and for Big Dave. Take care of him and Anne and take care of me here alone today. Please send plenty of airplanes for me to watch. Amen."

Anne and Dave exchanged understanding looks after that prayer.

"I'll run over to Mrs. Dawson's before we leave," said Dave. "I meant to do it last night and we got so busy I forgot."

Anne shut her lips firmly. "He'll be all right, I'm sure," she said with a smile and a little upward look.

Davey ate eagerly and finished first, then turned to Anne. "Where's the Book, Anne?" he said reaching out his hand. She smiled and produced from her apron pocket a little leather-bound book of the Psalms.

"Davey and I always read the Bible together before I leave," she explained. "Just now we're in the Psalms. Whoever finishes first gets to do the reading." She smiled at Davey tenderly. "If you don't mind we'll keep it up." She looked shyly toward Big Dave to see if he approved. "I've been thinking," she went on, "that what this place needs is a family. It's had several individuals living here at cross-purposes like a pile of jackstraws. There's nothing like reading the Bible and praying together every day to bring us all into one unit. If we can all look toward the Lord the first thing every day He will straighten out lots of tangles."

Dave agreed and listened eagerly as Davey read. Then right there over the toast and jelly, Anne spoke to the Lord quite simply committing them and the activities of the day into His care, praying especially for the invalids. She kept her head bowed a moment and suddenly Dave's voice broke the moment of silence. Hesitant and stammering, he said,

"Oh, Lord, thank You for saving me and bringing Anne and Davey here. I don't know how to pray but I want to learn, and I want You to show me how to glorify You all day, especially right here at home. Amen."

There was a gentle tender look on his face and Anne noted with a thrill of joy that he raised his eyes and looked straight into hers. He was humble enough not to be ashamed to pray with her. She wondered why she was so glad.

"Boy, oh boy!" sighed Davey in contentment, "it's going

to be swell here! Almost like having a home and a father
and mother," he added ingenuously.

Anne blushed furiously and dropped her eyes, then flashed
a look up at Dave and down again. She saw him still gazing
seriously, tenderly, straight at her and she blushed again,
rising quickly to clear the table.

They strung the hammock on the porch lest it rain, and
set a little table near the boy, with some of his books and
toys and a nice lunch wrapped in waxed paper.

"I'm going to ask Dr. Barnhart to look at him," said Dave
on the way in to town. "I can't help thinking it would do
him good to begin to use his legs more."

"I've wondered about that myself," said Anne. "I will be
glad to have another doctor's opinion. I think it may be wise
to transfer the case to him entirely, now that we're out here."

"It may be. In fact," suggested Dave, "why don't I stop
now and tell him that Davey is there? He might find time to
go up and it will make a break for the kid. He's only a block
or two out of the way."

The doctor was out but Mrs. Barnhart dimpled her mer-
riest and promised to tell him.

So it was that Davey had more than one caller that day.
Mrs. Dawson came about the middle of the morning and
made a nice grandmotherly fuss over him. Then Mrs. Barnhart came, with her daughter's two little boys. They stayed
for over an hour and Davey enjoyed every minute.

In the afternoon, Davey fell asleep until he was awakened
by the doctor's whistle.

Dr. Barnhart sat beside the boy for a long time asking
questions about his illness, going over him thoroughly. Finally he said:

"Davey, let's see just what those legs of yours can do. Put them down here. Now lean on my hand. There!" The boy's eyes were wide with startled wonder. Then fear seized him and he started to crumple.

"All right, back we go. That's enough for the first time," said the doctor pleased at the result of his test. "We are going to try this every day for a while. I think it won't be too long before you are up and around."

Davey howled with glee. Uncle Harry heard it and craned his neck to see what might be going on. Resentment flared anew over the strange cars and strange people that were making free with the house that belonged to his wife. Washing her dishes and stealing, yes *stealing* her jelly! Cookies or no cookies he'd got to stand up for his rights. It didn't look as if Dave was going to obey his order to leave. That man with the black bag, he must be a doctor. What right did Dave have to bring a sick boy out here? No telling what kind of disease he might have. They all might catch it.

The bitterness slowly heated itself up to a boil. At last it must have boiled over, for Uncle Harry took his faded cap and his pouch of tobacco and made his slow way down the hill to the bus. He and Aunt Amelia would have to take steps!

Chapter XXII

Davey greeted Dave with a whoop when he came with the first load of furniture on Wednesday afternoon.

They set up Anne's things in her room and she hung some soft white curtains that had been her mother's. Then it began to seem like home. Life had looked so very dark and difficult ever since her mother's death, it was hard to believe that bright things were coming her way.

Dinner that night was a pleasant time for the three young people, but Uncle Harry persisted in absenting himself.

He ate only two meals a day and he evidently planned to cook his own and eat alone, leaving everything for Anne to clean up before she could start getting dinner.

That couldn't go on, she decided. It was violating the family life that she was going to try desperately to establish. The very principle of the thing required that they all chip in together, whether of their money or their brawn or their privacy, for the common good.

But little did Uncle Harry care for the common good. He was busy at last, for the good of what he called the Mathers' rights. He had spent the day in the city. The results of his efforts would soon be manifest. He felt quite proud of himself. It was the first purposeful thinking and acting that he had achieved in years.

Davey was asleep and Dave and Anne were just about ready to call it a day when a car drove up through the June

228

twilight. They thought it might be Dr. Barnhart but there was no whistle accompanying the heavy steps.

A loud knocking on the door sounded ominous.

It was the postman with a special-delivery, registered letter. Dave signed for it with a puzzled frown. The name on the envelope showed that it was from a firm of lawyers. What now?

He tore the letter open and continued to frown. Anne watched him anxiously. She saw his face sag. The lines about his mouth settled heavily. Her heart sank. Everything had seemed to be going so smoothly.

He handed the letter to her.

"Uncle Harry's activities," he sighed.

She read it through but the involved legal phraseology left her bewildered.

"What's it all about, Dave?" she asked gently.

"It's a stew that Uncle Harry has stirred up," he replied wearily. "It looks to me as if he has hired a shyster lawyer to try to put us out of here. He saw I didn't take his threat seriously and he thinks he can scare me out this way."

"*Can* he put you out?" cried Anne, aghast.

"Oh, I don't think so. Certainly not after Dad gets home. That's the clever part. He says he's giving me three days. Let's see. Tomorrow's Thursday. Dad won't be home till Sunday. Clever chiseler! You see, I'm not the owner of the house and he is, in a legal sense, as long as Aunt Amelia is away. He represents her interest in the property, being her husband. If he can evict me before Dad gets home to fight him he thinks he has won. And of course what can Dad do in his present condition even if he is home?"

"But on what grounds could he put you out?"

"I suppose he told a lot of lies, which would have to be proved untrue by a lawsuit." Dave groaned.

They were silent several minutes.

Finally Dave said, "I'm too tired to think what is right tonight. I'm going to bed."

"I agree with you," said Anne. "Let's pray about it and in the morning it may look clearer. Remember how the Lord has ironed out other problems."

Dave nodded. "Yes, He can do it, there's no question about that. And if He wants me out, then out I'll go." But his voice betrayed his discouragement.

Anne laughed gently. "You say He can do it, but you think He has never been up against an Uncle Harry before?"

Dave grinned soberly. "Maybe that is about as far as my faith goes. Good night."

But Anne decided in the morning that when it came to faith, Dave far outstripped her. He came down to breakfast whistling and as cheery as ever.

"Don't tell me it's all ironed out already?" she gasped.

He smiled. "Why, I believe it is, yes," he replied in a pleasant even voice as he set Davey gently down in his chair. "I've realized that God knows exactly what He is going to do about it, and whatever He does is okay with me. I'm just going to stay here as long as He lets me. If this is where I should be, He will see that I stay here. If not, He has some other place. I think I can trust Him to see to Dad, too. He knows that responsibility better than I do."

Anne stared in awe. It all sounded so sensible and so perfectly in line with the Bible teaching she had always had, but when had she ever met anyone who really acted upon that teaching? More than ever she decided that this was the man she wanted to work for.

The fields were still sparkling with morning eagerness when Dave put Anne in the car to take her to school that morning.

He made the difficult turn through the stone gateposts and gave his usual exclamation of impatience at them.

Anne smiled in amusement.

"Why don't you take them down?" she asked wonderingly.

Dave stared at her and broke into a sudden laugh.

"Believe it or not, I never thought of it! I will. I guess there are a lot of things I could have done to make the place less dreary," he added with a sheepish look like a little boy who has had to admit that he really hasn't done his homework. "I seem to see a lot of things that I never saw before, now that you have come."

He lingered tenderly over the "you" as he spoke it and Anne was embarrassed to find that her cheeks were growing hot again. She turned her head away to hide her face. But her heart beat fast and the morning sparkle seemed brighter than ever. She turned back to cover the moment with a casual observation just in time to discover that Dave had been stealing a glance at her. She pretended that she hadn't caught his look. But there was such a sweetness about his lips "like a smile but he isn't smiling," she thought, that her heart did a somersault and made her words trip over each other.

Dave didn't answer the triviality yet the silence between them was not cold. It was a warm, thrilling living bond, almost too precious to touch with words lest it be shattered.

That afternoon when he picked her up at school she was ready and waiting expectantly. He smiled down at her contentedly as they started home. She made haste to try to cover her pleasure in his smile by talking about her school. But he seemed as interested in that as she, and still wore that contented, eager look. She scarcely dared wonder what it meant and whether the smile was for her. She made up her mind she was not going to be silly and get ideas.

Davey welcomed them lovingly and they set to work on the father's quarters. They brought Mr. Truscott's bed down from upstairs and put it in the wide bay window where he could see in three directions. They put his chest of drawers nearby, and a table. That was all he would need. They found a handsome old Chinese screen in a closet and dusted it off, placing it so as to separate his room from the rest of the dining room to some extent.

"He may not like being here in the center of things," said Anne, a little worried about making arrangements for a man she had never seen.

"I think he will," decided Dave. "He has fretted for years because there was never anyone around to talk to. He can't do much talking now, but at least he will enjoy what is going on."

Anne came in from her conservatory room with a small package and a paper bag.

"I brought these flower seeds and bulbs along. They were some Mother had saved. Do you suppose you could spade up a little garden on the sunny side of the house where your father and Davey can see the flowers? I think they will like to watch them come up."

"Sure thing," agreed Dave without enthusiasm. He tried to hide his reluctance. He had never cared for gardening, but if Anne wanted flowers, it seemed a small thing to do for her. He was terribly aware that board and room were hopelessly inadequate pay for what she was taking on. "We'll do 'er right now. How about it, Davey, want to watch?"

Dave was consistently cheerful these days and Davey

adored him. He carried the boy out and put him on a big thick blanket spread out on the grass. He propped him with some pillows from the sofa in the living room. The boy was overjoyed to be so close to the scene of operations.

Anne scurried around the kitchen getting dinner. Uncle Harry had not been in evidence all day. It was a great relief. He was certainly no help, and it was a strain to have him sitting around in disapproving silence.

He came in as she was calling Dave and Davey to dinner.

"Just in time, Mr. Mathers," she said cordially, as if no eviction letter had arrived. "We are all ready with dinner. Ham and hot biscuits. Does that sound good? Your place is set." She wanted to make sure he understood that they wanted him to eat with them.

But he merely stumped over to his old chair by the kitchen table and sat down, without a word. He took out his newspaper and started to read it.

The others went on with dinner, their happy laughter ringing out occasionally. Every time he heard it he would look up with malice in his dirty, yellowed eyes and settle down more stubbornly in his chair.

"Do you think it will be better to clean Aunt Amelia's little room while he is around, or when he's out?" asked Anne in a low voice as they ate their dessert.

"That's what I've been wondering. It's up to you. You seem to be able to handle him better than I. Personally, I don't think it makes much difference. He has made up his mind to dislike everything we do and whether he's here or away, it will be just the same. He doesn't actually stop us forcibly. I doubt if he could," Dave laughed.

"He could throw his pipe at me," giggled Anne. "But seriously, do you know whether we have the right to make changes without his consent?"

"I don't know why not," mused Dave. "Besides, he did give his consent, didn't he, that first night you were here and told him what you were planning?"

"Well, I took it for that. He didn't say no, and seemed to agree that he should have a room upstairs. In fact, from some of his sparse words I gathered that he had never wanted to sleep down here in the breakfast room, that it was all her idea."

"Okay, then go ahead. We are going to proceed with what seems to be right," he insisted. "We'll get to work on it Saturday."

"Do you know when Aunt Amelia is to come home?"

"No," replied Dave. "The last word was, not for a week yet. But I'm quite sure that if the hospital people can manage it, they will have her out the first possible moment."

They laughed.

"We had better be ready," Anne decided.

The next morning Anne was surprised to hear pounding and the smash of glass before she was up. She looked at her watch. No, she had not overslept. She sprang up and dressed quickly. Then she went in search of the sound. It had stopped and she called softly for Dave. He was nowhere in the house.

She stepped outside and looked around. She heard a banging again and there he was, up on the porch roof, working away at the sagging shutter. He had reglazed the broken window, too.

"Hi, early bird," she called gaily.

He grinned. "Hi yourself. Don't expect me to call you a worm. You look more like a butterfly." For Anne had put on a fluffy yellow organdy for the last day of school. Her eyes seemed to flutter up to his and then away.

"Soup's on," was all she could manage to say without her breath catching again. The bird songs were in her voice this morning.

"I'll be right in," said Dave eagerly.

At breakfast they discussed further improvements but each caught the other's glance several times and Anne felt her cheeks quite crimson.

"I'll mend that porch railing this afternoon," Dave planned. "I'm going to leave the lawn mower to be sharpened on our way in this morning, and we'll give the space right around the house a shave and a haircut."

Davey chuckled.

"Maybe we ought to get a cow or a goat," suggested Anne with a twinkle, "to keep the rest of the weeds down."

"Oh, *could* we?" pleaded Davey, catching at the enticing straw.

Dave smiled. "Well, I suppose we could have some kind of animal that would eat grass. I remember how much I always wanted pets. We'll see."

Davey's eyes shone with delight.

They hastily cleared away the meal and ensconced Davey in his favorite spot on the porch. He was not lonely, for his beloved model airplanes were a constant source of interest and the real airplanes put on a show for him by the hour. Besides, Mrs. Barnhart had promised to come every day.

But it was Saturday afternoon before she turned up again.

Dave was finishing the lawn and Anne had been planting the rest of her seeds.

"My, what a lot you have done," complimented the jolly little lady vivaciously. "This lovely old place takes to attention, doesn't it."

Dave looked at it appraisingly.

"I have never thought of it as a lovely old place, Mrs. Barnhart. I guess that's entirely my own fault. I have let it go when I could have done a lot to make it nice." He took off his old ragged broad-brimmed straw hat and wiped his forehead with his sleeve. "It's Anne who has given me some incentive and a vision of what it could be," he smiled. "In fact, I'm going to hate leaving it."

"Why must you leave it?" she inquired politely.

"Well, my uncle so heartily disapproves of us," he explained, "that he is trying to have me evicted. In fact, this is supposed to be my last day."

"You don't mean it," cried the goodhearted little woman raising her dimpled hands in horror. "Has he any right?"

"I think not." Dave sketched the status of the property.

"I shall ask my husband to get his lawyer friend to look into it immediately. That is outrageous."

True to form, she hastened away.

After she had gone, Anne looked wistfully about. Dave had just finished the lawn and they stood admiring the clean trim look of the place.

"Now for some paint, and it will have some self-respect again," planned Dave. They discussed the color, and decided that creamy white was best, to brighten the dark stone.

They started to stroll to the other side of the house. But as they came in sight of the driveway they noticed a car parked there. It looked vaguely familiar. Suddenly Dave stopped and gave a quick startled exclamation.

"Isn't that the sheriff's car, the one that was here that morning with the FBI man?"

Just then Davey's high voice could be heard calling frantically, "Anne! Anne! Big Dave!" and there he was on his knees peering through the porch railing, crying and waving to them.

Frozen panic in her heart Anne rushed to the steps.

How had the boy got out of his hammock and over to the rail? She forgot the car and the sheriff in fear for Davey.

But Dave did not wait for steps. He took three bounds and reached the porch, scaling the railing like a squirrel. He had heard the sound of hammering and intuitively he guessed what it must be. If the sheriff got his seal on the door who knows how long it might be before they could legally get it off?

Dave tore around the porch to the other side of the house where the main door was which he and his father had always used, for his aunt had seemed to prefer the kitchen end of the house.

There stood Uncle Harry, a wicked gleam of triumph in his eyes, and the sheriff was just about to pound the second nail into a board to bar the front door.

"Stop!" shouted Dave so suddenly that the sheriff jumped and dropped his hammer. Dave made a dart and grabbed it before either man knew what he was doing.

"Don't you know you are trespassing on this property?" demanded Dave. "Where is your warrant for what you are doing?"

The two men exchanged glances. Uncle Harry gave a mean little laugh.

"Don't you worry, we got it all righty," said the sheriff reaching in one pocket after another. As he searched he cast a suspicious glance at Dave. "Seems like I've seen you before, ain't I? Wasn't you the fella the FBI man picked up a week or two back? Heh! Heh! I thought so. We don't want no bad characters hangin' around these parts."

Uncle Harry stuck his muddy eyes almost into Dave's face.

"I always knew you'd come to a bad end. I been hearin' all about yer spyin'. You'll land in jail yet. Best place fer you."

Uncle Harry hadn't heard footsteps behind him, but all at once a deep voice boomed out,

"That will be enough. Sheriff, what's all this going on?"

Dr. Barnhart stood towering behind Uncle Harry. He looked as if he were ready to do battle with the sheriff himself.

"Mornin', Doc," said the officer genially. "This ain't a pleasant job, but these things hafta be done sometimes. This gentleman has had to have some undesirable characters put out of his house here."

"*His* house? Mr. Mathers, have you recently bought the property from Mr. Truscott?"

"Bought it? I didn't hafta buy it. It's been ours since Amelia's old man died."

"I understood that it belonged to both your wife and Mr. Truscott jointly."

"Oh yes. But he ain't here. He don't know what's going on here. I gotta stand up fer the rights and decency of the family. This here young upstart's been tryin' to take over the place. It cert'nly don't belong to him. He's got no right here. An' there's no tellin' when his dad'll be back, if ever."

All this time Dr. Barnhart's face had been growing more and more stern.

"Mr. Mathers," said he with suppressed rage, "Mr. Truscott *is* back. He is out in my car there now. You had better clear out. And you, sheriff, should have looked into this case before you listened to the lies of a chiseler."

Dr. Barnhart reached out and with one yank ripped the half-nailed board off the door.

"Sheriff," went on Dr. Barnhart, "I happened to hear the remarks made about this fine young man here, just as I came up on the porch. Any story about him, which by the way, is false, must have got out through you and nobody else. If I find that you are spreading any more tales about worthy citizens I shall see to it that proper measures are taken to relieve you of your office. Now leave the premises. I'm speaking for Mr. Truscott."

"Yes, sir. I'm leaving right now, Doc," the sheriff hastened to assure him.

But at last Uncle Harry had found his tongue.

He bared his ugly teeth and snarled at Dr. Barnhart.

"I'd like to know who you think you are," he hissed, "comin' in here and interferin' with the law."

"Man, you had better scram, or the law will interfere with you," the doctor flung at him. "Come on, Dave, let's get your father into bed."

"You can't do this, you can't—" barked Uncle Harry.

But Dave turned swiftly and picking Uncle Harry up by his collar and the seat of his baggy pants, with a twist of his arms he slung him like a sack across his shoulder and ran with him to the kitchen door, on the side of the house away from the drive lest his father see or hear him. Arrived at the back door he threw him onto his shaking feet and took his flabby shoulders and shook him till he dropped his pipe and his dirty teeth rattled together.

"Uncle Harry," he blazed, "I'll give you your choice.

Either you can shut up and behave yourself, and live like a decent human being with the rest of us or leave *now* and don't come back until you can."

Dave gave him a push into the kitchen and slammed the door. Then he ran back to the drive where Dr. Barnhart was waiting to help carry his father into the house.

"Let me do it, Doctor," he said breathlessly, his eyes still aflame with righteous indignation.

Gently he lifted his father and carried him into the pleasant airy dining room where his bed was already turned back and waiting.

A white-uniformed nurse with blondy-brown hair and a perky pink hanky in her pocket, stood by to assist.

Davey's wide eyes were peeking through the screen to see what on earth was going to happen next.

Chapter XXIII

After the patient was comfortably settled they went into the living room to talk it all over.

Big Dave carried Davey lovingly in and kept him on his lap.

"Do you know, little brother, that you did a fine job of warning us today, and saved us a great deal of trouble?"

Davey beamed. "I just didn't like the looks of that man," he said. "And I was afraid to yell right there, so I stood up like Doctor Barnhart taught me and I walked a couple of steps. But then I had to crawl."

"It won't do him any harm?" asked Dave anxiously.

"I think not," said the doctor, "but he should rest a while, before he does any more."

"Okay, fella, to the hammock you go for a while."

Dave carried him out and he was soon fascinated with his airplanes again.

When Dave came back he said, "Now tell us, Doctor, how you happened to arrive at the right moment."

"I was in the hospital making my rounds this morning and I saw that your father was feeling unusually bright so I decided that it would be good to take advantage of it. Then we met my wife on the way up the hill. She called me out of the car and told me your predicament. It's the Lord who times such things as that, you know. I'm glad I had a chance to squelch that sheriff. A man like that in office is a menace. I've known of his dealings before. But he knows that I know and he's afraid of me. He won't try anything else, I'm sure. But tell us, what have you done with your uncle? Thrown him down the drain?" The doctor chuckled.

Dave was unusually serious as he told them.

"I hope I didn't do something the Lord would not approve of," he said slowly. "It seemed the perfectly natural thing to do, at the time, but I'm afraid maybe I was angry."

"I think you had every reason to be angry. Didn't you know that 'God is angry with the wicked every day'?" People get the idea that God is a wishy-washy sort of person who is always smoothing things over. He is far from that."

Dave looked up hopefully.

"Is that true? I'm so glad. I've been troubled ever since I did that to Uncle Harry."

"I don't see anything terrible about it," said the doctor. "He earned it."

"Yes," agreed Dave solemnly, "but when I think of what I've earned, and how God has forgiven me—"

"But Dave, don't you see the difference? You have repented. He has not. God can forgive because Jesus Christ took the penalty of all sin, but unless a person really hates his sin, he doesn't even want forgiveness."

Dave breathed more freely. "That makes it better, sir. I sure don't want to disobey the Lord."

As he looked up, Dave happened to glance at Anne. He surprised an adoring look on her face which she quickly snatched off and hid. But Dave kept his gaze on her, wonderingly.

The doctor saw and smiled to himself.

"There's something else I'd like to ask you, Doctor," went on Dave after a moment. "Why is it so many, sort of impossible, unusual troubles have turned up since I was saved?

I always thought that it was the people who weren't Christians who were supposed to have the tough time."

"Theirs comes after this life," answered the doctor sadly. "For Christians He gives this message: 'Beloved, think it not strange concerning the fiery trial which is to try you, as though some strange thing happened unto you, but rejoice, inasmuch as ye are partakers of Christ's sufferings.' I've never known a person to take a forward step with the Lord that the devil didn't make a fuss about it."

Dave thought a moment. Then he spoke reverently.

"That seems to place us on a very high plane, sir," he said seriously. "You mean you think the devil stirred up all this mess? I thought it was punishment on all of us because we have been so rotten mean to each other all these years."

"But the rottenness of a sinner calls forth all the more of God's grace! And when we repent He can overrule anything we have done. Yes, I think Satan had something to do with your difficulties. I think he would like to tempt you to think that God has forsaken you and that all your new life and joy are a mirage."

"Hm-m!" said Dave thoughtfully. "In that case, I feel honored."

The doctor bowed his head then and prayed such a prayer of thanksgiving and trust that there were tears in all eyes when they looked up.

They wandered out to the car, and the doctor stood a moment giving last directions to Anne about the care of her patient.

"Look!" cried Anne. There was awe salted with humor in her voice.

Down the hill toward the bus line stumbled a slight, stooping figure with a pipe in its mouth, trudging stubbornly over the stony path, weighed down with two bulging old suitcases.

"Pitiful!" declared the doctor. "But how right!"

Dave nodded solemnly.

The doctor drove off, stopping to pick up the pathetic old man on his way.

Dave and Anne walked up to the house. They had the feeling that they had climbed a difficult mountain together.

"I wonder what Doc will say to him," mused Dave.

"Whatever he says, it will be just right. Didn't the Lord iron it out, just as you said!" remarked Anne joyously.

"Did He *ever!*" answered Dave with a smile. "I'm going to keep on praying, though, for Uncle Harry. Somehow I feel as if he'll repent some day, when he gets to the end of his rope."

"That will be the day!" said Anne fervently. "Well, I must get in now to my patient." Anne was all business, now that the excitement was over.

Dave looked down at her, noting her fresh white uniform. She saw his look and colored, anticipating a teasing remark.

"I got this," she explained apologetically as she smoothed it down, "because I thought it might make the patients feel more at ease if I looked sort of professional."

But he was not making fun of her. He continued to gaze at her until she blushed again.

"It looks nice," was all he said, but his look made her heart sing.

Mr. Truscott slept some time. They had finished lunch, and Anne was busy about his little section of the room when she realized that his eyes were open and upon her. He looked puzzled, as if he were trying to reconcile this attractive young nurse with the middle-aged woman he had expected. But whether he was pleased or not he gave no sign. Nor did he give any evidence that he noticed any changes about him.

"He wouldn't," said Dave with a sour grimace.

"Well, anyway, I guess we are free now to fix up Aunt Amelia's room," she said happily.

And so they spent the rest of the day moving and scrubbing and running in betweentimes to see to Davey and the father.

It was a disgusting job, but a very satisfying one to get at that room that Uncle Harry had been occupying. There was dirt everywhere and soiled clothes that must have been lying on the floor for months. Anne would not have been surprised to find a nest of mice in the old shoes kicked into a corner under the bed. Poor Aunt Amelia with her arthritis had not cleaned under there for nobody knows how long.

Monday afternoon Dave took the enormous walnut bed apart and carried it upstairs section by section. Then he spent some time making stilts for a single bed so as to raise it high enough for Anne's convenience.

At last Aunt Amelia's room was ready. It had flowered chintz curtains at its one little window; a gay pink geranium stood in a pot on the wide window sill, the walls were a soft rose color, the white spread was spotless. Dave had made a real cupboard with doors instead of the makeshift closet, and the last thing they did was to paint the floor a shiny gray.

Once in the thick of the work Anne came upon Dave standing by a window reading an old newspaper. He had a peculiar expression on his face. She looked over his shoulder as he pointed to a yellowed photograph heading a front-page column.

"That," said Dave in a tone of disgust, "is the—the *bliz-zard* I thought I cared about. How would *she* ever stand up to a situation like this?" He waved a hand at the room.

Her little jeweled swords seemed to glitter gaily even through the newsprint, those swords that had cut into his life so cruelly. What a deliverance!

"Thank God," he murmured softly.

"What did you say?" asked Anne.

"Oh, nothing," he sighed. "I was just being thankful that—" he turned and looked squarely at Anne—"that *you* are here and not *that* girl."

"Oh!" said Anne in a small voice, afraid to trust herself to speak. Then she added, "She is very beautiful."

"You think so?" scorned Dave, glancing once more at the picture. "I used to, but that kind of beauty is only skin deep." He turned again and looked straight into Anne's eyes. "Why," he said tenderly, "I'd rather watch that pretty pink come up in your cheeks and see the sparkle in your eyes than all the jeweled Darla Dartmans in the world." Then he gave a teasing little chuckle. "That-a-girl! Color them up again."

Anne's dusty hands flew up to hide her burning cheeks, but she couldn't conceal the light in her eyes. She laughed and tried to look down but her eyes would keep turning up to see whether Dave was still looking.

"Brother! I'm glad it's you!" exclaimed Dave again.

"So am I," replied Anne in almost a whisper. "There, I think I hear your father stirring. I must go." She dashed away, leaving Dave to wonder why she had rushed off like that.

Before Friday came, Anne was exhausted. She had tried to divide her time between the cleaning and the cooking, Davey and Dave's father. When she got so weary she could not stand up she would go in and sit beside Mr. Truscott. Sometimes she would make pleasant little remarks, sometimes she would read to him. He spoke rarely, and then his speech was not clear. It seemed to be a great effort. But she soon noticed that his eyes seemed pleased when she read the Bible to him. She read again the Twenty-third Psalm which Dave had read in the hospital. The patient opened his eyes at once and listened all the way through and then he smiled. It was the first smile that had made its way through the bitter crust of his hard heart in many years.

So she often read that, and the Gospel of John. Once, when she was reading the words, "whosoever believeth on the Son hath everlasting life," he tried to raise his hand to stop her, she thought. But he made a great effort and finally succeeded in making her understand: "Read that again."

So she read it again, and watched his face.

"Again." His lips made the shape of the words.

Once more she read it slowly. He drew a deep satisfied breath.

"Good," was all he said, and fell sound asleep.

Anne ran to Dave with the news when he came home and together they rejoiced.

Then came Friday and Aunt Amelia.

They heard her before they saw her. The ambulance had not been able to make the entrance, and the orderlies had put her in one of the canvas carrying bags instead of a flat stretcher.

"Just like a corpse!" she ranted.

And all the way up the drive as they stumbled over the rough uneven stones with their heavy burden, she swore at them. Her coarse, deep bass voice bellowed through the afternoon sunshine.

Davey heard her first from his roost in the hammock, and called Anne.

She had the patient taken into her rehabilitated room and put to bed. Then she went about deftly doing the little things that make sick people feel they are cared for.

Aunt Amelia followed her with eagle eyes. At last the woman could contain herself no longer.

"Well, what's your name, nurse?" she demanded.

Anne smiled her sweetest. "Just call me Anne, if you like," she replied.

"That's easy. I hope you're going to be more efficient than those worthless nurses in the hospital. I'm not going to pay a cent toward your wages if you're not. I told my nephew I couldn't afford a nurse but he insisted. By the way, I had a husband here when I left. Where is he?"

Anne started guiltily. But it was not her story to tell.

"I haven't seen Mr. Mathers around for some time," she said. "Would you like a drink now?"

"No."

"Will your doctor be out to see you today?"

"No. I told him not to come any more. If I need anybody I'll get one out here. Cheaper. I wish you'd go and get my husband. Tell him to come right away. I want him."

Anne drew a deep breath. She might have known that would come soon. She slipped out of the room as if she were going after him.

What could she say to stall this woman off? Oh, if only Dave would come. And then she heard his whistle.

"She's there," she told him breathlessly, "and she wants her husband. What'll you do?"

Dave grinned. "I'll tell her what I did."

"Oh!" cried Anne. "What'll she do to you?"

"What can she do?" He laughed. "Kick me with her leg in a cast?"

He marched into his aunt's room whistling.

"Well, Aunt Amelia, it's good to see you back. You're looking tops. How do you like your new pink 'budoor'?"

"Dave Truscott, who paid for this, I'd like to know? I've sent that little girl for your uncle. I'm sure he didn't do this. Now you might as well tell me the truth. What's going on here?"

Dave smiled genially.

"That's just what I came to tell you, Aunt Amelia."

He sat down on the edge of her high bed and told her the whole story from beginning to end. Every time she tried to interrupt he overrode her. And she was too amazed and fascinated to stop him.

"And so, I told him off. I said if he couldn't live like a decent person, he could get out and not come back until he could."

Dave was calm and unperturbed during his recital. Now he sat waiting for whatever storm might come. Anne was listening from the kitchen.

Amelia Mathers raised herself as well as she could on both elbows and looked her nephew straight in the face.

"David Truscott," she began in her war-horse voice, "I've always thought you were a worthless good-for-nothing boy, but I've changed my mind. That was the finest thing you ever did." And then much to Dave's discomfiture, her left eyelid drooped and it was all he could do to restrain himself from a fit of abandoned laughter.

"I'm glad you think so, Aunt Amelia," he said with a chortle. "Now I think you will be pleased, too, with the nurse we have. She is very capable, but you must remember that she is not an ox. Be reasonable. If you're not, you can't have her, that's all."

"She's pleasant and willing enough," responded Aunt Amelia, tersely. "As for her being efficient, I'll wait and see. Now you can go. I'm going to sleep."

Dave went into the kitchen and closed the door. He saw Anne hiding there behind the refrigerator and he grabbed her hands gleefully and they did a silent jig together.

It was a full two weeks before Aunt Amelia gave her decision about the new nurse. The week had been full of constant errands, so much that Anne sometimes thought her feet would drop right off her body. Aunt Amelia sometimes seemed to try her out to see how much she could stand, but Anne and Dave had agreed to keep in constant prayer about the matter so that she would be able to keep her temper.

Dave's father was greatly improved. He was able to take a few steps and he loved to edge to the porch and watch Davey on his new swing. A gentle smile was beginning to mold his features into softer lines and his eyes followed Anne about tenderly.

At twilight on the Friday evening two weeks after Aunt Amelia had come home, Dr. Barnhart made one of his regular visits to his "hospital on the hill" as he called it, for the old woman had actually been willing to accept his services.

He was in her room, announcing that in a few days she was to try a step or two.

Anne was hovering about and Dave had had Davey out for a stroll on his shoulders around the grounds. They came in just as Dr. Barnhart was about to leave.

"Wait, Doctor," called Dave from the dining room. "We have something to show you."

Footsteps came toward the little breakfast room, and there

was Davey, walking toward them, holding tightly to Dave's hands above his head.

Anne's face shone.

"Oh, praise the Lord," she sang under her breath.

They all exclaimed, even Aunt Amelia. She had taken a notion to the boy and always insisted that Anne make sure that he had enough cookies.

While they were rejoicing, other footsteps, slower and more hesitating, approached from the dining room. They caught their breaths in wonder.

Like a ghost from the past came Jason Truscott, into his sister's room with a solemn smile.

Tears and smiles greeted him as he went straight to his sister's bed.

"Mele," he said, calling her by the brother-and-sister name he had used to use so many years ago, "I'm sorry—" He broke down and sobbed and then Aunt Amelia took his hand and stroked it.

"So am I, Jase." She quavered through unaccustomed tears.

There wasn't a dry eye in the room. Then in the little embarrassed pause that came, Amelia raised herself up again and pointed to Anne, but she spoke to her nephew.

"David Truscott," she announced, "there is the finest nurse in all this county, and I want to pay her whole salary on one condition, and that is that you do what you haven't had sense enough to do so far—marry her!"

Anne's cheeks flamed crimson and she covered her face. But Dave took one step to her side, and cried joyously as he folded her close to him:

"Aunt Amelia, that is exactly what I intend to do, if she will have me." He looked down into her radiant face so trust-

ingly turned up to his and right there before them all he set
his lips reverently on hers.

In mock solemnity Dr. Barnhart walked over to a calen-
dar that hung on the wall.

"Let's see," he said, putting on his glasses. "I believe I pre-
dicted this development in one month. You have anticipated
me by one day. Let me congratulate you, Dave."

Davey almost shouted, "Boy, oh boy, I thought you two
would never wake up and get any sense!"

They set the wedding for the last day of June. The minister from the little church at the foot of the hill was invited
to perform the ceremony, and all the Barnharts were to be
there.

The living room was dressed in the fine old lace curtains,
whitened and starched, that had belonged to Dave's grand-
mother. ·

Mrs. Barnhart made the wedding cake herself.

"You're going to wear my white crepe wedding dress, you
know," she lovingly insisted to Anne. "I could never get into
it again if I wanted to." She chuckled.

Davey proudly stood by on his own two feet to hand his
new brother the wedding ring at the proper moment.

Aunt Amelia went completely berserk financially and had
a florist send palms and a big box of pale pink roses.

"That's what she looked like to me," she told Dave gruffly,
"when I came home and saw her blush every time you
looked at her."

At that, Dave had to take his old despised aunt in his arms
and hug her till her eyelid drooped again from sheer amazement.

After the ceremony when Dave was putting Anne lovingly

into the old jalopy, it seemed as if he could scarcely bear to leave her long enough for him to walk around to the other side of the car.

The scratched fender had been carefully touched up for the week-end wedding trip; the old stone posts were no longer; the white trim gleamed, clean as chalk lines; and green grass and flowers softened the dark outlines of the house.

They paused a moment looking off at the sunset place over the pine-rimmed valley.

"If I had only known, all the dull years in this dreary old dump, what God was planning," said Dave drawing Anne close to his heart.

His lovely bride smiled up at him and glad tears came into her eyes.

"If *I* had only known, all those anxious days in Pearl Street, and the nights when I worried so!"

"You know," he reminisced tenderly, "I had the strangest feeling when I first went to the house on Pearl Street, as if something wonderful was about to happen. And it did! I found a jewel that day, a wonderful pearl—on Pearl Street!"

Dear Reader:

We would appreciate hearing from you regarding the Ruth Livingston Hill Classics. It will enable us to continue to give you the best in inspirational romance fiction.

Mail to: Ruth Livingston Hill Romance Editors
Harvest House Publishers, 1075 Arrowsmith, Eugene, OR 97402

1. What most influenced you to purchase **JEWELED SWORD?**
   - ☐ The Christian Story
   - ☐ Cover
   - ☐ Backcover copy
   - ☐ _____
   - ☐ Recommendations
   - ☐ Other Ruth Livingston Hill Classic Romances you've read

2. Where did you purchase **JEWELED SWORD?**
   - ☐ Christian bookstore
   - ☐ General bookstore
   - ☐ Other
   - ☐ Grocery store
   - ☐ Department store

3. Your overall rating of this book:
   - ☐ Excellent ☐ Very good ☐ Good ☐ Fair ☐ Poor

4. How many Ruth Livingston Hill Romances have you read all together?
   (Choose one) ☐ 1 ☐ 2 ☐ 3 ☐ Over 3

5. How likely would you be to purchase other Ruth Livingston Hill Romances?
   - ☐ Very likely
   - ☐ Somewhat likely
   - ☐ Not very likely
   - ☐ Not at all

6. Please check the box next to your age group.
   - ☐ Under 18
   - ☐ 18-24
   - ☐ 25-34
   - ☐ 35-39
   - ☐ 40-54
   - ☐ Over 55

Name _____

Address _____

City _____ State _____ Zip _____